on track ...
Gentle
Giant

every album, every song

Gary Steel

sonicbondpublishing.com

on track ...
Gentle
Giant

every album, every song

Gary Steel

sonicbondpublishing.com

Sonicbond Publishing Limited
www.sonicbondpublishing.co.uk
Email: info@sonicbondpublishing.co.uk

First Published in the United Kingdom 2020
First Published in the United States 2020

British Library Cataloguing in Publication Data:
A Catalogue record for this book is available from the British Library

ISBN 978-1-78952-058-3

Typeset in ITC Garamond & ITC Avant Garde
Printed and bound in England

Graphic design and typesetting: Full Moon Media

Thanks and gratitude to

Composer James Gardner for decades of conversation on the finer aspects of unpopular music and in particular, technical pointers and advice on this project; and fellow Antipodean Gentle Giant fan David Maclennan for his much-valued input.

Friend and songwriter Peter Kearns for informing me of this opportunity, and Stephen Lambe at Sonicbond for publishing it.

Gentle Giant for providing such a rich and enjoyable source of repeated musical pleasure (and the odd challenge).

David Knight for graciously availing me of his 'in concert' pics of the band.

My incredibly patient, understanding wife, Yoko, who did her utmost to keep the children out of my man-cave during the preparation of this book.

Five-year-old Minay whose favourite band is 'The Gentle Giant' (but whose favourite singer is Taylor Swift) and her brother Lunay, whose appreciation of Gentle Giant's polyrhythms is entirely instinctual.

on track ...
Gentle Giant

Contents

Prologue

Mum bursts into my room with a look of sheer panic on her face. 'Gary, what in the blazes was that? Which window is it?'

It's 1973, and her 14-year-old son has just put the needle down on his newly purchased import copy of Gentle Giant's *In A Glass House*.

The sound of glass breaking that begins (and ends) the album is a rare example of Gentle Giant using the *musique concrète* technique. But unlike the 1940s French experimental composers who manipulated raw sounds to form an integral part of their compositions, on *In A Glass House* it's used mostly for its shock value. Sure, the sounds are echoed and merged into the beginning of 'The Runaway' and are thematically linked to the album's concept, but it's the sheer impact that resonates.

Mum was extremely house proud, with every little trinket lovingly displayed and dusted, and vacuuming dutifully taking place twice a day. As an angry adolescent, who blamed the older generation (my parents) for all the ills of the world, I would take any opportunity to torture her with 'my' music, all of which she hated with a passion. 'Mind-bending', she called it; this new progressive rock from bands like Emerson, Lake and Palmer, Henry Cow and King Crimson. Born in 1929, to strict Methodists, even Bing Crosby was a bit risqué for her.

By late 1973, I had already subjected her to a variety of musical torments as I went through my personal rock revolution, from the raw-throated vocal stridulations of Janis Joplin to the taunting acid rock of The Doors' Jim Morrison. There was so much for her to hate! But progressive rock was something else. Because it was influenced by European art music, sometimes it was really pretty and even classical sounding. However, that was all a ruse, because it generally preceded some monster riffing and some killer 'heaviosity'. And here's the thing: the dynamic contrast between the pretty, soft, mostly acoustic parts and the heavy electric sections, was extreme. With the volume turned up to eleven, to better hear the quiet acoustic sections when the inevitable hard rock riffing came bursting out of the speakers, the dynamic contrast was mindblowing.

The suburban drama described above took place in the context of a lower-middle-class nuclear family in the provincial backwater of 'Mother' England's most far-flung colony: Hamilton, New Zealand. Back then, sheep outnumbered humans by about 20 to 1, but Hamilton was dairy country with its peaty soils and its research facility conducting experiments on cows that would have made the hair on Frankenstein's neck stand to attention. Our green and placid land may have seemed more suited to folksy gatherings, country-rock and the kind of old-timey roots stew personified by Bob Dylan's backing outfit, The Band. And it's true, there was that, but the music fiends at Hamilton Boys' High School were mostly adherents of the burgeoning glam scene, while to me, it was progressive rock that was impossibly alluring.

Progressive acts seldom made it down to the bottom of the known world, and certainly not so-called second division bands like Gentle Giant who often had to make do playing support. Jethro Tull played one date in our largest city, Auckland, just on the cusp of their great progressive satire, *Thick As A Brick*, and Rick Wakeman performed a less than well-received outdoor rendering of *Journey To The Centre Of The Earth* with the Auckland Sinfonia in 1975, but that was about it.

Instead, I relied almost totally on music weeklies like *Melody Maker* and *NME*, which arrived three months late, and necessitated a very serious devouring of every word and scrap of relevant information. It was in *NME* that I had noted the name of a band I wanted to check out. They never got much more than a mention, but this Gentle Giant, they sounded just like my cup of tea. And when *In A Glass House* turned up in the local record shop's tiny import section, I had to blow my newspaper delivery savings. I mean, it had a window built into the cover itself with profiles of the band etched into the 'glass'. Cool! And it was on the Vertigo label with its great roster of underground acts. Excellent!

And it was. But here's an admission. As much as I was intrigued, and adored parts of it, there was also something about *In A Glass House* that, at the age of 14, I found impenetrable, and beyond my immature powers of perception and understanding. Plans to further investigate Gentle Giant's music were scuttled by the so-called punk rock revolution, which I stupidly bought into, wholesale.

Meanwhile, my obsession with those music rags led to something of a career. For 40-plus years now, I've been writing about music. But with thousands of album reviews and interviews in the can, in the early 1990s, I started to re-connect with my adolescent prog-rock past and was amazed to discover worlds within worlds within worlds of exciting, challenging, virtuosic and intensely creative music. This wasn't nostalgia beckoning, but a re-investigation into something I wasn't done with, and in the case of Gentle Giant, hadn't been quite ready for the first time round. I duly acquired all the group's albums and over time, found that Gentle Giant was becoming one of my all-time favourite groups.

This book is my tribute to a band that clung on for an amazing ten years despite an almost blackly comic series of management and record company botch-ups, pumping out eleven studio albums and performing countless gigs in the UK, Europe and America. It's impossible not to respect these guys for the sheer bloody-mindedness of keeping on keeping on, despite what was most often a tepid response by the marketplace. I'm so glad they did because their legacy – their music – has enriched my life. And no matter how many times I listen to those records, they never grow stale on me.

Gary Steel

PS. Oh, and Mum? If you can somehow hear me from the cosmos, please accept my humble apologies for my appalling adolescent behaviour.

Introduction

Imagine what it would look like if Gentle Giant were just starting out now, in the 21st Century. The PR machine would go into overdrive hyping up the constituent aspects of the group that make them so immediately identifiable: the arcane influence of medieval and renaissance music, the counterpoint a cappella singing, the rampant multi-instrumentalism and changing onstage roles. In short, Gentle Giant would sound like a gimmick dreamt up by a publicist after too many chardonnays and then superimposed on an unlucky gang of rockers by a record company who would then straitjacket them into the purgatory of sales-driven sameness, never giving them the chance to experiment and spread their wings artistically.

I mention this because – when you put it in black and white or try to explain them to a friend – those most immediately recognisable elements of Gentle Giant's music do make them seem like a gimmick. And yet, in the atmosphere of wayward experimentation that existed in the late 1960s, it was possible to exploit a seemingly incompatible (not to mention archaic) musical style and mix it with underground rock flavours to create a fusion that was beyond the reductive, superficial grasp of the PR guff merchants – not to mention over the heads of the rock scribes of the day.

Which I guess is my way of saying that the particular set of circumstances that enabled the formation and unflagging creative impetus of Gentle Giant to exist during the 1970s – the zeitgeist that for a time at least, put them in step with the then-nascent rock underground – simply couldn't have happened at any other time. Which isn't to say that the group is time-locked and hopelessly marooned in the 1970s, because as much as they're very much of their time their music eclipses the era in which it was born, and amazingly, seems to sound fresher with each passing year.

That's why there's been a renaissance in activity around Gentle Giant in recent years, leading to several of their albums getting the Steven Wilson surround sound remix job and their music getting name-checked in academically-oriented avant-garde magazines like *The Wire* and even sampled by numerous hip-hop groups. Check out Madvillain's 'Strange Ways' for its steal from 'Funny Ways' or Level Zero's 'Lootpack' for its steals from 'Playing The Game', just for starters.

And there, in a nutshell, is the grand irony: that in their own time, Gentle Giant was somehow never part of the inner circle of progressive rock groups and never got close to achieving a hit record; that even after years of touring graft they were often reduced to playing second fiddle to vastly incompatible touring mates, and that few published rock histories give them their dues. In fact, there's even a so-called progressive rock tome that fails to mention them! But that now, two decades into the 21st Century, Gentle Giant are suddenly somebodies and their music rehabilitated so that longtime fans can refresh their interest in this great body of work and new fans can experience them as if they were happening right now.

It has been surmised that the beginning of Gentle Giant's problems was the fact that they'd formed around the core membership of 1960s psychedelic pop'n'soul confection, Simon Dupree And The Big Sound, and it's probably true that this caused a credibility problem for the group. The new hippie underground of the late 1960s and early 1970s was ideologically opposed to packaged and commercialised pop groups and treated them with contempt, and the fact that the three Shulman brothers (drummer Martin Smith joined late in the piece) had been the nucleus of one such group won't have gone down well. Credibility was crucially important in 1970, and Simon Dupree and The Big Sound just didn't have any.

I suspect, though, that it was Gentle Giant's interest in early music that did them in with the tastemakers of the day, rather than their previous incarnation. The music press in the early 1970s had an influx of writers from underground hippy magazines like *IT* and *Oz* who seemed to suffer some kind of cultural cringe when it came to music that was intrinsically English in origin.

Rock itself had grown out of an American music form, R&B, which was itself a blues hybrid. The British blues boom of the mid-to-late 1960s once again transplanted an American music form into a UK context, and many of the musicians involved in that scene went on to mainstream success in bands like The Yardbirds, Led Zeppelin and Fleetwood Mac. Folk music was largely seen an American music form – something Bob Dylan did – while the innovators reviving English folk music (Bert Jansch, John Renbourne, Davey Graham) were roundly neglected.

Classical music was considered part of the European tradition, so when groups like Procol Harum and The Nice started playing around with classical influences, that was considered permissible. But aspects of English folk culture like Morris dancing were endlessly pilloried and satirised, and you can see this attitude to the rich, mystical folk (pre) history of England in the way the Monty Python crew portrayed the Arthurian legend in the 1976 film, *Monty Python and The Holy Grail*.

This partly explains why Gentle Giant's interest in early music hobbled their credibility with UK audiences influenced by those very important music magazines, while to American audiences the incorporation of elements of medieval and baroque music forms as well as early folk music seemed impossibly alluring.

It's worth mentioning at this point that several other groups in the early to mid-'70s plied their versions of early English folk and medieval music, but that none were as artistically successful. Steeleye Span were responsible for a fairly brazen rocking up of folk traditions, and later, Gryphon stole some of Gentle Giant's thunder by rocking up medieval music. Neither of them used the techniques to make tenacious or spectacular new music from old traditions.

Another issue may have been the band's origins in Portsmouth, which was hardly a hotbed of cool rock. One gets a sense of the lack of respect accorded small regional towns by the naming of the Portsmouth Sinfonia, an aggregation of non-musicians who recorded several albums in the 1970s of proudly incompetent renditions of well-known classics. Featuring amongst their ranks composer Gavin Bryars and electronic music guru Brian Eno, the orchestra was an extended joke, and while their music is entertaining, they're hardly the best advertisement for Portsmouth as a seething hub of creative music activity.

But really, we'll never know quite why Gentle Giant never ascended to the lofty commercial heights of Yes, Emerson Lake and Palmer or Genesis, and because it's a done deal and we can't go back and create an alternative reality where they're phenomenally successful, we're not going to dwell on that fact in this book. It's likely that their problem was a bit of all of the above, but more importantly, that they just weren't lucky when it came to hooking up with the right management or record companies or tour management. While at times their incessant touring of America paid dividends, more often than not they ended up on double bills with completely incompatible acts and audiences that were violently opposed to their intellectual take on rock. It's on the record that in the early days, they ended up on a stadium gig with Black Sabbath where someone let off a cherry bomb, Phil swore at the crowd, and the group were roundly booed offstage. Another time, they weathered a double-act with Steeleye Span performing to just 32 people.

And we can't let it go without mentioning that they weren't the easiest band to get into. Try playing a song by Yes or Genesis, and compare it to Gentle Giant. Those two bands were both lush and symphonic and, arguably, were making a kind of pop music. For all their entertainment value – and Gentle Giant were great entertainers – their music was unforgivingly complex and riddled with musical puzzles. And like King Crimson, their music was edgy and didn't shy away from dissonance. It's notable that after King Crimson's innovative and successful 1969 debut, *In The Court Of The Crimson King*, that after losing Greg Lake to Keith Emerson's new band – Emerson, Lake and Palmer – the group went through what was arguably its most fertile period between 1972 and 1974 with the albums *Larks Tongues In Aspic*, *Starless Bible Black* and *Red*. And that like Gentle Giant, they struggled to pull in the punters, finding a more interested and ardent audience away from England.

So, what is it 50-odd years on from their debut album that makes Gentle Giant worth revisiting? And what is it that makes them so different from their peers? Although Gentle Giant was infected with the zeitgeist surging through post-psychedelic underground music in the early '70s, they stand apart from much of what was going on at the time, in crucial ways. The infamous liner note from *Acquiring The Taste* that maps out their intention to go where no band has gone before and to experiment to their heart's content, had more than a grain of truth, although it was by no means unique, and this spirit of experimentation was rife amongst progressive rock bands at the time. The liner notes said:

It is our goal to expand the frontiers of contemporary music at the risk of being very unpopular, we have recorded each composition with the one thought – that it should be unique, adventurous and fascinating. It has taken every shred of our combined musical and technical knowledge to achieve this.

That statement has been critiqued as naïve and even pretentious, but as a mission statement it perfectly sums up what Gentle Giant undertook to achieve in its early years, and I view it as both brave and a little sardonic. It could also be said that while the group, right from the start, boasted a somewhat unique approach to musical structure and that their sonic signature was also identifiable, that their music wasn't immune to influence, especially on the first few albums. Like King Crimson's Robert Fripp, Gentle Giant were masters of the giant riff, and like Fripp, they knew how to write and play those mean, 'evil', often minor-chord riffs in a hard-hitting and dynamic fashion, often bursting

15

out of a quiet passage with explosive dynamics. Furthermore, guitarist Gary Green, whose strength was his ability to play across an astounding diversity of styles, was also capable of Fripp-like flurries and arpeggios.

Some of the group's more rollicking, physical grooves aren't far removed from Jethro Tull circa their most successful album, *Thick As A Brick* (1972) and that group also have a tendency towards a folk-influenced troubadour style that's a real feature of Gentle Giant. Finally, the influence of the great Frank Zappa is obvious on several Gentle Giant tunes, together with a similar approach to composition-as-tuned-percussion.

It's interesting to note, therefore, that Gentle Giant toured with King Crimson, Frank Zappa and Jethro Tull in the early '70s, and that Kerry, Derek and Ray have all stated their appreciation of Zappa in interviews. Zappa returned the compliment. Famously acerbic about contemporary ensembles – especially English ones – in a mid-'70s interview he named Gentle Giant as one of his favourite groups.

But really, seeking to find in Gentle Giant some invisible connection to other musicians or bands leads nowhere. As others have pointed out, of all the 1970s groups Gentle Giant were the most hermetic, despite the fact that they led a largely nomadic life on the road where one would expect them to have fraternised with other bands.

One of the most bizarre aspects of Gentle Giant's existence is the total lack of collaborations outside of the context of the band, and the rarity of guest turns on their records. Where King Crimson's Robert Fripp collaborated with the likes of Brian Eno and David Bowie, there's no record of any member of Gentle Giant performing outside of the band. And where it was *de rigueur* for progressive rock bands to release solo albums along the way, there was never any talk of that happening with Gentle Giant, either. And apart from a few random musicians having been employed to add instrumental parts to specific songs on their early albums (including producer Tony Visconti) there are few guest shots on their albums. The notable, glaring exception are the uncredited backing female singers on one of the band's more regrettable songs, the funky 'Mountain Time' on the latterday album, *The Missing Piece*. Still, given the fact that Gentle Giant toured so relentlessly and performed alongside many other bands on these tours, it's astonishing that no musical associations were formed at any time during the group's ten-year lifespan.

One can surmise endlessly about the reasons behind all that, but the most feasible explanation is that Gentle Giant were *tight*. They were clearly on a mission, and given their relatively lowly status in the pecking order, it must have taken a high degree of discipline, perseverance and unflagging energy to keep this thing going, year after year, with often two albums appearing within the space of a calendar year and a gruelling series of tours in between. There seems to have been an almost missionary zeal to the project, and it's apparent from songs like 'Funny Ways' that they felt very much on the outer – outside of convention and charting new territories and a new 'Way Of Life'.

Had Elton John – who performed with the Big Sound towards the end of that group's lifespan – joined the Shulman brothers in Gentle Giant, then perhaps their entire trajectory (not to mention the music) would have been utterly different. But as it happened, former Royal College Of Music student, keyboardist Kerry Minnear was recruited, and the rest is history. Minnear's specific interest was baroque and medieval music and Gentle Giant was an opportunity to explore those techniques in a contemporary context. The Shulman brothers enabled that passion by becoming passionate enthusiasts themselves and helping give voice to the canny fusion.

But here's the other crucial factor: Gentle Giant were the all-singing, all-playing, mostly all-writing ensemble. They just didn't need outsiders. Because their processes meant that they operated on near-democratic principles, perhaps they just never felt the need to indulge their artistic flights of fancy outside of the group name. They certainly existed in a time of almost unlimited musical freedom, especially from their 1970 debut until the advent of punk rock in 1976 and their slow decline as market forces made survival more difficult.

That the three Shulman brothers (two of whom were in the band after 1972) had grown up together and knew each others' musical capabilities well, must have meant that there was a friendly competition but also respect and trust. That the Shulmans were capable players – on a multiplicity of instruments – and writers, is without doubt, but it's their long-term collaboration with Kerry Minnear that really made Gentle Giant the musical force that it was.

The Shulmans had grown up in a musical family (their dad was a part-time jazz musician), and by the time Gentle Giant was formed, they'd already had extensive gigging experience in what started out as a school band, Simon Dupree and the Big Sound. Reputedly a sweat-soaked, high energy, soul-flecked R&B aggregation, their recordings were compromised by management, who wanted to turn them into pop stars. Largely recording cover versions and achieving hit single status with a song they vehemently hated – their radicalised psychedelic take on 'Kites', a song written by the composer of 'Itsy Bitsy Teeny Weeny Yellow Polka Dot Bikini.' Despite a five-year contract with EMI, by 1969 the tides of fashion had changed yet again and it was obvious that the band wasn't going to fly with the emergence of the new underground rock scene. Hence, they took time off to rethink and come up with a new project with a new name: Gentle Giant.

It's informative listening to Simon Dupree and the Big Sound in light of what came later. While there's little of the character that would define Gentle Giant in their music, it's clear that this is a very competent working band, and it's this work ethic and ability to do whatever is required that laid the groundwork for the Shulman brothers' next enterprise.

It's easy to understand how the hip new underground would have looked down their noses at Simon Dupree and the Big Sound, however. Only The Beatles, it seems, was able to survive the transition from pop to stoner rock band because they were in an unassailable position, having established their commercial and critical dominance over a period of time in which their credentials as players and writers was beyond dispute. Unlike a regularly gigging band – the fab four had by this stage long given up performing live – The Beatles were able to self-determine their future and call the shots. The Big Sound were simply not in this privileged strata of rock royalty.

Looking back through the long lens of history, however, there's a lot to like about Simon Dupree and The Big Sound, and though there's nothing obvious in the sound to connect them with the group the Shulman brothers formed in 1970, it's there all the same in several different ways: in their 'the show must go on' sense of bravado and professionalism, and the muscular, sweat-drenched aspect of Gentle Giant's music. You'd be a crazy person to claim that Gentle Giant's music was directly influenced by soul and R&b, but nevertheless, it's embedded in their approach, especially to live performance.

Although the Shulmans got to write b-sides and album tracks in the Big Sound, it wasn't until they dumped the old band, auditioned new players and met and mingled with Kerry Minnear that something really special happened, and the powerful fusion that was Gentle Giant mysteriously coagulated. Somehow, the collaboration really worked. Minnear was a studious, somewhat quiet chap who was not only something of a gifted keyboardist but who held a special fascination for tuned percussion.

In concert footage of Gentle Giant, Ray and Derek Shulman come across as confident, playful and boisterous, while Kerry seems somewhat fey, but is clearly almost surgically implanted into the rhythmic matrixes of the group's sound. And ultimately, this is the thing that makes Gentle Giant greater than the sum of its parts: the way it all works together as an organic machine, with all the corresponding parts perfectly in sync, the members having recognised their duty to do exactly what they're supposed to do to serve the music.

It's not a subject that's fulsomely discussed on the various Gentle Giant-oriented message boards, but unlike every other progressive rock group ever, soloing and improvisation weren't accentuated. It's an important point and one that deserves further discussion. Yes, there were long solo turns during live shows on certain songs, and let's not forget that a drum solo was obligatory at every gig back in the '70s. But compared to other progressive rock groups, the length of their songs was determined mostly by compositional elements.

Where the complexity of many progressive rock groups is partly around extended soloing or written parts for specific instruments, Gentle Giant's complexity essentially stems from the writing. Seldom is one individual instrument left to extrapolate, but instead, it's the way the instrumentation and the voices lock-in together that makes it what it is.

This isn't to claim that in a performative sense Gentle Giant are not virtuosic, but that unlike so many groups of the era, there's not the sense that they set out to grandstand or impress. Instead, it's all about the music and the way the voices, keyboards, guitar, bass, drums (and whatever else is being played) serve the composition.

Kerry expounded a little on the way the process worked in a 1976 interview:

If a song is written with a certain section, the mood is chosen first by the writer. Then he gives us the parts. If I've written it, I'll give the guitar part to Gary Green as I hear it, the bass part to Ray, try to get the right feel on the drums from John Weathers, and the vocal we leave until last. It's normally a question of reproducing what the inspiration was. After a few plays, though, they start adding their own little quirks… but that's good because we're a group, not an orchestra. We're not there to play someone else's music, we're all a part of it.

It's also important to point out that their structural differences stem from the early music techniques that make the group sound so different in the first place.

So, what of those medieval and Renaissance influences and the resultant techniques used in the music of Gentle Giant? Let's briefly examine those techniques, and the impact they had on the music.

The single most overt technique is counterpoint, where instead of a typical melodic line becoming the main element of 'the song', the piece has two or even more melody lines simultaneously moving in different directions, note for note. This explains the way the instrumentation in Gentle Giant locks together and works as a kind of exploratory puzzle with micro-melodies flinging themselves around and keeping us, the avid listener, on our feet.

Counterpoint, which hit its apex with that great innovator, JS Bach, creates a space where no individual melody is necessarily dominant, but if you listen carefully, the melodic line played on one instrument might be echoed or further examined on another, but in a different way; or there might be melodies played on one instrument that works against, or provide contrast with, the melodic lines of another. Many artists use counterpoint, but no one in the popular arena (or in unpopular progressive rock) used it as extensively and interestingly as Gentle Giant.

Another fascinating technique used extensively by the band is hocketing, a technique where a musical phrase is divided up between several different instruments. But it's polyphony – a singing technique from the Middle Ages – that is perhaps the most instantly recognisable vocal technique used by Gentle Giant. This is where two or more vocal lines work simultaneously against each other, and also translates to instrumentation. Related to this is the canon, another distinctive aspect of the Gentle Giant vocal approach, where multiple voices sing a line but start at different times, thereby creating a bizarre 'echo'.

It's fascinating that Gentle Giant use techniques from both the Middle Ages and the Renaissance period, given that in medieval times there were strict rules around what was allowed in music (even down to notes that were considered evil); rules that were later trashed by Bach and his successors.

While the group often used exceptionally tricky time signatures, it's interesting to note that for the most part, they stuck to a 4/4 metre, and then devised how to have fun with divisions therein. This kept a strong pulse and helps to explain why John Weathers was their most successful drummer, as his 4/4 pulse freed the others up to explore ways to create mindboggling manoeuvres.

The group were masters of polyrhythms and poly metrics, where several contrasting rhythms might be patterning at the same time on different instruments. These might seem like mere techniques on the printed page, but they were used not just to impress but to create a palpable strangeness, and sense of difference, to the music itself. Gentle Giant music is often busy – some might say fiddly – but just as often, it's quiet and elegant, which again goes against the supposed excesses of progressive rock. In fact, one of the hallmarks of their sound is that they can go from a rabid frenzy of cascading notes and changing time signatures to an absolutely, heart-stoppingly gorgeous moment, all on the head of a pin. Consequently, repeat exposure to their albums is necessary for the myriad layers to sink in and make sense.

So, to recap, it's the compositions themselves, and the way the band perform the compositions, that makes Gentle Giant what it is. While that could be said to some degree about other progressive rock bands, it can also be claimed that Gentle Giant are one of the genre's least indulgent, most concise bands.

One other key aspect of the group's music is the fact that so much of what they did is built around rhythm. With a group like Genesis, there's firstly a sense of melody and secondly a sense of sonic architecture – sheets of sound. Gentle Giant are quite different. When does percussion become a sequence of notes, and when is a melody, a riff? There are so many fast, interlocking sequences, and so much of it is percussive, to one degree or another.

It's not surprising that once Gentle Giant had hit on its core membership, they then stuck with it to the end. When John Weathers joined in 1972 it all fell into place: suddenly, they had a master of rhythm who had a powerful style; one that didn't add to the complexity, but simply ploughed through the music with an innate sense of swing that helped everything gel. That was important because Ray Shulman was never going to be a typical bassist. Taking a leaf out of the Jack Bruce school, Ray could hold down the rhythm essentials but really shone when he was using the instrument as a lower-octave guitar, contributing melodically and contrapuntally as he picked out the notes.

Kerry Minnear's keyboard contributions were integral. They helped to form the exoskeleton of their music, as well as a large percentage of the actual *sound* of Gentle Giant. Although Kerry was never a showy player like an Emerson or a Wakeman – both of whom he has criticised for their excesses – he took advantage of the multiplicity of keyboards becoming available in the 1970s, and can be heard playing a variety of synthesizers, pianos and organs as well as the Mellotron. In live footage of the group, Kerry's stack is impressive but is modest compared to the keyboard titans of the day.

Gary Green's guitar-work was like the secret ingredient that each meal needs to send it off the scales, and his special talent seems to have been knowing exactly what was required and when. Much has been made of his blues background, and that's especially apparent on the early albums, but it's his incredible versatility and ability to come up with the perfect sound or melodic phrase that defines his work with Gentle Giant.

And then there's Derek Shulman, whose distinctive vocals and overall presence reinforce the sense of physicality about the band. Those who were lucky to witness Gentle Giant live, attest to their strengths in this arena, and there's a strong sense from the band themselves that their recordings never quite captured this aspect of the group: five hairy, sweaty men on stage going for it.

Finally, there's the way that all five members of the group work together, and their onstage multi-instrumentalism. That both Shulman brothers were adept at a range of instruments, as was Kerry, meant that they could get close enough to performing the songs like the recorded versions. In fact, the group have claimed in interviews that the albums were mere 'drafts' for the main event – the live experience. The fact that one minute Kerry would be at his keyboards and the next sawing away at an electric cello or performing a vibraphone solo, or that Ray would swap his bass for a violin and Gary his guitar for a recorder made for an entertaining spectacle, but it was more than that.

In 1973, an eighteen-year-old guitarist, Mike Oldfield, had a huge hit with *Tubular Bells*, a continuous track on which he layered himself playing a variety of instruments. Did the fact that he had laboured over all the parts himself make a difference? Would the album have been as distinctive had he hired studio guns to achieve the same thing? In fact, it's the sense of struggle that gives *Tubular Bells* that special quality, and the slightly hesitant and just slightly out of time moments, as amateur as they might seem to some, have a charm that the piece would never have achieved had it been performed by a professional orchestra.

The same applies to Gentle Giant. In the studio, the parts are played perfectly, because they were able to perform a track until they got it right, or to overdub specific parts. Live, with the slight delays as they move from instrument to instrument, facing technical hurdles as they go, there's a real sense of the challenge they've set themselves and it comes across in the energy of the music itself. It's there in spades on the

group's one official live album of the era, *Playing The Fool*, on which
the arrangements are at times radically altered from the studio versions.

Unlike most of their contemporaries, Gentle Giant's discography
doesn't represent a mess of lineup changes and reunions. Apart from
the dull thud of too many grey-area live albums that have surfaced in
recent years, the group's output is mostly confined to the tidy collection
of eleven studio albums they released in their short, ten-year lifespan.

It's one of the real enigmas about Gentle Giant that they knocked
it on the head in 1980, and have never been tempted into a reunion,
and that none of the former members has gone on to do anything
particularly notable musically in the public domain. The nostalgia
industry is huge and there are so many once-great artists hitting the
road one more time despite – in some cases – much diminished
performative abilities. At the time of writing, I see that there's an event
called FrontMan3 featuring members of The Hollies, 10cc and The
Sweet, none of whom were original or essential members of those
bands. So big respect to the collective force that was Gentle Giant for
having had the balls to know when it was time to quit, and move on. In
a bizarre coincidence, FrontMan3/10cc vocalist Mick Wilson is one of
the members of post-Gentle Giant group Three Friends with Gary Green
and Malcolm Mortimore.

The Early Years

Any assessment of Gentle Giant necessarily starts with the Shulman brothers, who were the core of the band, and the only members (apart from John Weathers, who joined the band much later) to have already had extensive on-the-road and recording experience.

Born in Glasgow, Scotland but raised in Portsmouth, England, there were five Shulman siblings: Phil, Ray, Terry, Derek and sister Evelyn, all of whom became adept and versatile musicians. If this seems odd at a time when working-class children would seldom have been encouraged to invest time or money in the arts, they undoubtedly had their father to thank. While he was a salesman by day, Shulman senior was a jazz saxophonist by night. Consequently, the terraced house was always buzzing with music and the children got all the encouragement they needed to pursue their combined interest in the field. Their parents insisted that they practice for at least an hour each day, and Ray was already adept at guitar, violin and trumpet by the age of ten.

Derek and Ray's school band, The Howling Wolves (named, of course, after the great blues vocalist Howling Wolf, otherwise known as Chester Burnett) ultimately evolved into Simon Dupree And The Big Sound, the fictional 'Simon Dupree' almost instantly becoming a millstone around Derek's neck.

It's instructive to learn just how quickly Derek and Ray came to be 'semi-pro' musicians – which undoubtedly kept them from the drudge jobs so many would-be pop stars took on to keep the (howling) wolf from the door. Older brother Phil was eventually persuaded not only to join the group (which soon became The Roadrunners) but also to take up the saxophone specifically to do so. By the time of the line-up that would come to be known as Simon Dupree And The Big Sound in 1966 and the management and record deal that would come with the name, the three Shulmans were already seasoned live musicians, and four years battling it out live and in the studio during the tumultuous late 1960s will have given them all the experience they needed to meet the forthcoming challenges of Gentle Giant at the turn of the decade.

Simon Dupree And The Big Sound – Part Of My Past (2004)

If you've ever wondered about the origins of the big, beefy and surprisingly soulful sound that underpins Gentle Giant – especially in live performance – then look no further than this compilation, which gathers together just about everything by the Shulman Brothers' previous venture.

Although Simon Dupree And The Big Sound were shoe-horned into a variety of pop styles that they weren't entirely comfortable with, as the name suggests the group was originally modelled on large soul/ R&b ensembles like Zoot Money's Big Roll Band and live, they were reputedly a hot and sweaty proposition.

We'll probably never get a proper taste of Simon Dupree And The Big Sound in concert, but reputedly, they were a much more wayward and propulsive proposition than the recorded version. It's clear from the excellent double CD compilation *Part Of My Past* that the group, for whatever reason (or perhaps multifarious reasons) allowed themselves to be force-fed management-led changes to their musical style and sound, and listening to their recorded output between 1966 and 1969 can be a confusing experience. Ironically, this stylistic confusion is somehow reminiscent of the various stylistic cul-de-sacs Gentle Giant found itself in from the late '70s as it thrashed about trying to please everyone and pleasing few, least of all themselves.

What we hear on *Part Of My Past* is firstly an adept but rather stereotypical soul/R&B band who then get shoehorned into trendy psychedelia, and subsequently, Love Affair-style exponents of pop balladry.

Part Of My Past is far from essential for moderate Gentle Giant fans, but it reveals Derek, Ray and Phil's first 'proper' band as a better-than-average mid-to-late '60s pop group, and for dedicated Gentle Giant fans it's certainly of great interest to explore the Shulman's early recorded work. There's no hint of any leaning towards progressive rock on these two CDs – which compile their singles, their one (1967) album, and a never-released 1968 album project that had been provisionally titled *Once More Unto The Breach Dear Friends*. But neither can it be completely disregarded or discarded, as it's definitely a step on the way to the great things the three Shulman brothers did only a few years later.

It's certainly interesting that while most progressive rock bands had blues backgrounds, the Shulman brothers' early sound, by contrast, was sautéed in propulsive rock'n'soul.

Disc 1

'I See The Light' (John Durrill, Michael Rabon, Norman Ezell)

The group's soul circuit sound is upfront on their first single, a cover of the Five Americans' hit, released in December 1966. With its burbling organ and stereotypical vocal, this minor hit sounds like dozens of other bands of the pre-psychedelic era but captures the band in a blazing performance.

'It Is Finished' (Paul Smith/Evelyn King)

The same warm organ, a trumpet fanfare and an almost unrecognisable pop'n'soul vocal from Derek, form the basis of this b-side on a song co-written by BBC producer Paul Smith and the Shulman brothers' older sister, Evelyn King.

'Reservation' (Albert Hammond)

This second single was hastily recorded and well received. But assessed against the psychedelic revolution that was starting to take shape by its release in February '67 it already sounds a bit out of its time.

'You Need A Man' (Paul Smith/Evelyn King)

Another b-side featuring the Smith/King (nee Shulman) songwriting partnership, this is a perfectly competent but fairly predictable slice of soul/R&b.

'Day Time/Night Time' (Mike Hugg)

An inexplicably re-titled interpretation of Manfred Mann's 'Each And Every Day', 'Day Time/Night Time' tanked, despite its memorable chorus, melodic pop structure and pleasing arrangement (harmony backing vocals, horn fanfare).

'I've Seen It All Before' (Paul Smith/Evelyn King)

Another b-side, co-written by Evelyn King, the Shulman brothers' sister, 'I've Seen It All Before' once again features prominent, Alan Price-like organ and a propulsive R&B sound. It's pretty good, really, but by May of 1967, this must have sounded a bit old-hat.

'60 Minutes Of Your Love' (Isaac Hayes/David Porter)/ 'A Lot Of Love' (Homer Banks)

A medley from the group's first album, released in August 1967, must have been geared towards hinting at the sweaty soul routine the group gave off in their live shows. It's okay, and if the vocals had been as distinctive as say, Eric Burdon (of the Animals), there may have been a point of difference.

'Love' (Edwards)
The same can be said of this rather laboured cut from their album.

'Get Off My Bach' (King/Shulman)
Here's a rare piece co-composed by Ray and his sister, Evelyn, and it's interesting only insofar as it deviates from the strictly R&B sound to poke the borax at a love interest who 'doesn't dig the stuff that I play' in an almost comedic fashion.

'There's A Little Picture Playhouse' (Hine)
With its rollicking piano and brash horns, the group are here moving towards that specifically English style of dandy, vaguely satirical pop of which The Kinks were the kings, on a song composed by the group's keyboardist, Eric Hine. Derek's vocals are clearly recognisable, as he's not emoting in a laboured soul fashion, for a change.

'What Is Soul' (Gallo/King)
An unnecessary cover of a Ben E. King song, its inclusion on the group's debut album is kind of sad, but typical of an era in which it was standard for pop groups to dot their albums with cover versions.

'Teacher, Teacher' (Dupree/Shulman/Shulman)
The first example of a Shulman brothers' composition (Derek undercover with the Simon Dupree nom de plume), 'Teacher, Teacher' is a titillating piece of pop whimsy that's like a more innocent Benny Hill. Given that this piece of (rather amusing) fluff was recorded the same month the Beatles' epochal *Sergeant Pepper's* was released, it's hard to picture just where their heads were at.

'Amen' (Cooke)
Recorded to imitate a live party with what sounds like a Caribbean rhythm, it's not quite as infectious as they probably imagined it to be.

'Who Cares' (King/Shulman)
The last track from the debut album is another co-composition between

Ray and his sister, Evelyn King. It's a pleasant enough pop/soul crossover but errs on the side of cliché.

'Kites' (Lee Pockriss/Hal Hackaday)
The Shulmans vehemently dislike the song, their one bona fide hit (number eight in the UK charts), but taken on its own merits, it's an entertaining piece of flower power whimsy, and it's fascinating to hear Derek singing in a completely different style. With its 'mysterious' mallets and Mellotron and exotic female monologue, 'Kites' may have been a completely concocted wee conceit, but it works a treat. Don't forget that for every 'White Rabbit' (Jefferson Airplane) there was a silly (but entertaining) psychedelic embarrassment like The Rolling Stones' '2000 Light Years From Home', and while 'Kites' comes from the silly end of the psych spectrum, it's still a classic of its type.

'Like The Sun Like The Fire' (King/Smith)
Marking a distinct change of style, this track by the group's regular writing partners is a kind of orchestral pop psychedelia (with some nice horns and reeds) that ends in a circus-like flurry of horns. They're sounding 'mature' on this memorable and detailed arrangement. Given better luck, this could have been a hit.

'For Whom The Bell Tolls' (King/Smith)
This 1967 single is a kind of wimpy, semi-acoustic psychedelic ballad with wafting Mellotron and Derek giving his best poptastic vocal performance. It's perhaps a little too derivative for its own good.

'Sleep' (Dupree, Hine)
Co-written by Derek and the group's keyboardist Eric Hine, this is another hymn-like, vaguely orchestral ballad with violin, trumpet and an emotive vocal performance. It's as hard to pin a style to it as it is to figure out what they thought they were doing.

'Part Of My Past (King/Smith)
This song has pretty Mellotron on its flute setting and parping trumpets on a pop-ballad style that sounds like a Bee Gees offcut, right down to the vibrato on Derek's vocals. It's actually rather nice, though, and hard to understand why this January 1968 single release bombed so badly.

'This Story Never Ends' (Hine/Shulman)
A big lush pop ballad with horns and vibes that is written by band members Eric Hine and Ray Shulman.

'Thinking About My Life' (Shulman, Shulman)
Derek and Ray co-compose this orchestral pop/soul hybrid with its dramatic flourishes and its lost-for-words 'la-la-la' chorus. There's real craft here, but it's a song in search of a hit, an exercise in pop. Another single flop.

'Velvet And Lace' (Shulman, Shulman)
Another compositional credit for Derek and Ray that can be seen as their own private class in songwriting upskilling. There's a bit of Mellotron, but this is a kind of late '60s lush pop that's a real shift from either the soul/R&B of their early sides or the psychedelia that preceded it.

'We Are The Moles' (Shulman, Shulman)
Presented in parts one and two, 'We Are The Moles' is the most intriguing oddity included on *Part Of My Past*. The story goes that, increasingly frustrated that they were being ignored, Simon Dupree And The Big Sound released this piece of wonky psychedelia as The Moles in an attempt to get a clean slate with critics and radio programmers. Unfortunately, none other than Pink Floyd's Syd Barrett revealed to the media that The Moles – who some even thought were The Beatles in disguise – were, in fact, The Big Sound, and it flopped. Given that the group had already left the psych sound behind by this point, it's intriguing to conjecture whether this was what the group really wanted to be doing. Or was it simply a big joke, with its processed vocals and needle-point guitar sound and those silly lyrics: 'We are the moles and we stay in our holes hiding our faces revealing our souls.' Regardless, both parts are a lot of fun and the Shulman's expert fake psychedelia isn't so far removed from XTC's perfectly crafted psychedelic facsimile on their 1980s project, Dukes Of The Stratosphear. In fact, that group recorded a tribute called 'The Mole From The Ministry'.

'Broken Hearted Pirates' (Miki Antony)
A brazen piece of pop pomp overlaid with seagull cawing. Over-orchestrated, with a mad middle section featuring a military band, it's hard to understand why they chose this tune to cover, as the band are

as good as submerged. Stranger still, this single features Dudley Moore on piano.

'She Gave Me The Sun' (Shulman, Shulman, Shulman)
The first time all three Shulman brothers get a composition credit, and it's a solid attempt to write a pop-ballad anthem with a few unexpected instrumental flourishes. But ultimately, it comes across as overkill.

'The Eagle Flies Tonight' (Hazard)
Obviously still taking advice from their management, this is another over-orchestrated pop ballad where the band gets lost under the bombast. Hundreds of bands were making this kind of pop in '68 and '69 in a craven attempt to hit the charts. It was another single bomb.

'Give It All Back' (Shulman, Shulman, Shulman)
And now, for something completely different: suddenly, they're a funky-ass rock band with a Shulman brothers song that, while it's musically mainstream, has character and a set of lyrics that distinguishes itself. This is probably the first time that the Shulman flavour reveals itself in full, with its short but Gentle Giant-like wonky horn manipulation and humorous lyrics and grunt. It features pre-fame Reginald Dwight (Elton John) on piano.

Disc 2
'Stained Glass Window' (Grady, Zekley)
Another cover version that's way out of character and shows just how schizophrenic the Big Sound had become in its endless search of a hit. Still, this harpsichord-laced song – reminiscent of American vocal groups like The Turtles and The Association – shows just how adept the Shulmans already were at vocal harmonies.

'Please Come Back' (Shulman)
A lovelorn pop ballad with a rather gorgeous horn-led minor-key melody, this sounds like a pretty good b-side. Composed by one or more of the Shulman brothers.

'Light On Dark Water' (King, Smith)
Back to the songwriting partnership of the Shulman's sister Evelyn and BBC man Paul Smith, again this echoes the Love Affair-like ballad style that was all the rage in '68/'69. It ain't half bad.

'What In This World'

Another harpsichord-led track with Mellotron doing its fluty thing and a rather dull love lyric. It's simply bizarre to hear Derek sing in this style. It seems to have no writing credit.

'What Cha Gonna Do' (King, Smith)

A Mellotron-laced, lovelorn pop ballad with a horn flourish that's straight out of *Magical Mystery Tour*, and a big-balled vocal performance from Derek. This song was apparently the idea on which 'Part Of My Past' was based.

'Don't Make It So Hard (On Me Baby)' (Parker, Floyd)

Oddly, this cover of a 1966 Sam and Dave tune, regresses to a pseudo-soul ballad style, but the lashings of Mellotron and big bass give it a flavour that's nicely contradictory to Derek's vocal, which is so steeped in R&B that he could pass for an Afro-American.

'Kindness'

A buoyant faux-psychedelic novelty with Beatles-style chord progressions, violin and xylophone interjections. 'It don't seem fair/ can't find no kindness anywhere'. It has no writing credit.

'Castle In The Sky' (King, Smith)

Another Mellotron drenching with typically dainty harpsichord filigree and a yearning pop lyric about a better world that is surely beckoning.

'Loneliness Is Just A State Of Mind' (King, Smith)

Why they were still bending over to perform such rote examples of late 1960s pop by this stage is a question that will probably never be answered. With its strummed guitar, Mellotron and Derek's pained, almost Tom Jones-style vocal, it's all just a bit too much... or too little.

'Laughing Boy From Nowhere' (Shulman, Shulman, Shulman)

Beginning with what sounds like a laughing chipmunk but is actually Phil's son Damian, the arrangement has a few quirks that one might expect from the Shulmans but its core is a kind of dull '60s pop that's simply too obvious. It features Reg Dwight/EJ on piano, who was depping for Eric Hine while he recovered from glandular fever.

'You' (Shulman, Shulman, Shulman)

Starting with a trumpet fanfare and moving into another song that sounds like something Tom Jones might have attempted on a b-side, unfortunately there's nothing particularly 'Shulman' about this pat and ordinary piece, which features Dudley Moore on piano.

'Can't You See' (Shulman, Shulman, Shulman)

It's as if the Shulman brothers, given the chance to compose their own material, have used it as an excuse to explore the machinations of pop songwriting rather than to innovate. In other words, to learn their craft. This horribly commercial piece could be one of those off-Broadway groups like Fifth Dimension, and it's a brash and clichéd song, which again features pianist/comedian Dudley Moore.

'Now' (Shulman, Shulman, Shulman)

Once again, this sounds like something written for some kind of brash Broadway show. Had these early Shulman songs been flogged in the US to the right people, maybe their career path could have been completely different.

'Rain' (Shulman, Shulman, Shulman)

Ditto this very orchestral piece with jingle bells and 'bum-bum-bum' female backing vocals. 'Rain, rain, come again, another day'. Etc. This makes perfect sense in an environment in which the Fifth Dimension were having hits with songs like 'Up, Up And Away', but... Again, it features pianist/comedian Dudley Moore.

'Something In The Way She Moves' (James Taylor)

A James Taylor song that's transformed from his maudlin folk into standard pop fare, here.

'I'm Going Home' (Elton John, Bernie Taupin)

One of the more intriguing songs on the album is this collaboration with Elton John, before he was famous, on what must have been one of the first EJ/Taupin songs recorded. His piano playing and vocals are clearly heard here, to the point where you wonder: where was the Big Sound during this session?

Gentle Giant (1970)

Personnel:
Derek Shulman: lead and backing vocals, bass
Phil Shulman: trumpet, saxophones, recorders, lead and backing vocals
Ray Shulman: bass, guitar, violin, triangle, backing vocals
Kerry Minnear: Hammond organ, Minimoog, Mellotron, piano, tympani, xylophone, vibraphone, cellos, bass, lead and backing vocals
Gary Green: guitar, backing vocals
Martin Smith: drums
Paul Cosh: tenor horn
Claire Deniz: cello
Produced at Trident studios, August 1970 by Tony Visconti, engineered by Roy Thomas Baker
Release date: November 1970
Running time: 37:00

First albums tend to be one thing or the other: either a slam-dunk exposition of everything that's great about a band or artist, or two sides of vinyl that merely hint at what might lie in store if you stick with them as they grow creatively. In the former category, we have King Crimson's epochal *In The Court Of The Crimson King* (1969), and Emerson, Lake and Palmer's self-titled debut (1970), both of which are statements of intent and a blueprint for what came later. The latter category includes *Yes* (1969) and *From Genesis To Revelation* (1969), neither of which was particularly indicative of the future direction of either Yes or Genesis, or could even hint at their evolution to their respective peaks, *Close To The Edge* (1972) and *Selling England By The Pound* (1973).

Gentle Giant's self-titled debut was something altogether different. While the group are clearly still feeling their way towards the pinnacles represented by their greatest period (1972-1975) and have yet to develop many of their defining musical characteristics, *Gentle Giant* remains a great – if highly variable – box of proto-prog wonderment, a veritable Pandora's box of open experimentation defined by the expansive mind-set of the year in which it was recorded.

Who would have thought that four of the band's six members had only months before been plying their wares with the compromised pop'n'soul of Simon Dupree And The Big Sound? There's not even a hint of that band in Gentle Giant's big, bold debut, which can still elicit sonic and musical thrills 50 years later. However, the dogged determination and on-the-road experience of that earlier band certainly

33

show on a record that never sounds tentative.

Listening to *Gentle Giant* with fresh ears after all this time, it's hard to understand why it created barely a ripple in the underground rock scene of 1970, because it's a record with many powerful moments that is packed with audacious moves along with just a few minor missteps; and those missteps are characteristic of the experimentation of the time, and thus very much part of the territory. The only assumption to be made is that the music press (who were a crucial component in getting the music across to consumers) knew about the Shulman brothers' history in the commercially oriented Simon Dupree And The Big Sound, and that in their eyes the group lacked rock credibility. 'Rock cred' – whatever that really means – was seen to be vitally important in the wake of the psychedelic revolution.

They certainly had everything else going for them. Gentle Giant were signed to the terminally hip Vertigo label, the underground rock imprint of Philips, which would go on to become one of the most collectable labels of all time along with Harvest and Charisma. What's more, the first album was produced by Tony Visconti (who'd come to them fresh from David Bowie) and engineered by Roy Thomas Baker, both of whom would go on to stellar careers behind-the-scenes. The album also had a distinctive cover design by George Underwood, an artist/musician whose artwork graces many other albums, including those by David Bowie, T. Rex and Procol Harum.

The record has been lambasted frequently over the years for its sound, but there's nothing especially wrong with its sonics and, blasting from a good stereo, there are thrills to be had. Perhaps what its critics really mean is that Gentle Giant hadn't quite coalesced. Ultimately, it's an album that's of sporadic rather than sustained brilliance, and one that – for all its musical delights – is just the first step in Gentle Giant's creative development.

And although its members had experience in the studio, this is the first time they'd been given free rein to experiment, were less than sure about how to best harness the studio as a creative environment, and reliant on Tony Visconti's experience with multi-tracking and other technical studio boffin procedures to get what they wanted. Visconti paints himself in interviews about the recording as a key creative input, and that may well be true. But Gentle Giant were eager and adept learners.

'Giant' (Shulman, Shulman, Shulman, Minnear)

Like all the tracks on *Gentle Giant*, 'Giant' is credited to the three

Shulman brothers and Kerry Minnear, but the song is believed to have originated with Ray. The group's recorded life begins with a swelling, churchy organ that instantly brings to mind Deep Purple's Jon Lord, before a propulsive, guitar-like bass introduces an exciting, simmering horn-led melodic figure and the most guttural vocal Derek Shulman ever put on vinyl. Where Derek's later lead vocals were distinctively shorn of vibrato, on this one occasion, he's to be heard emitting his lines in an impassioned voice that resembles Joe Cocker's gargling-on-whisky Woodstock performance, but which is even closer to the bleating, raw-throated sound of Family's Roger Chapman.

The lyrics tell the story of the birth of a giant, and his ascendancy in the world, so it's a literal/mythic introduction to the band and its imagined conquest of the music world. As such, it's an explosive intro that bares some musical comparison to label-mates (and future touring buddies), the jazz-rock group Colosseum. Another recognisable influence is Frank Zappa, who the band greatly admired, and tricky, Zappa-like horn lines and metric trickiness abounds – although the track is simple compared to the sometimes mindboggling complexity of their later work.

There's a bit of everything here, from ethereal, phased organ to the majestic Mellotron/choral segment. While it's merely an entrée, many of the qualities associated with Gentle Giant – the explosive dynamic, the unstoppably great riffs, the unusual combination of intelligence and physicality, the slight awkwardness – are already on board.

'Funny Ways' (Shulman, Shulman, Shulman, Minnear)
One of several songs from *Gentle Giant* that would remain for many years in the group's concert repertoire, 'Funny Ways' is the first real inkling of their interest in early music. And with Ray's delicate violin intro – both plucked and bowed – and gorgeous, troubadour-style vocal by Phil, the first impression is that it wouldn't sound so out of place in an Edwardian parlour. That is until the band kicks in for a powerful declamatory chorus sung in a typically strident voice by Derek Shulman.

This signature Gentle Giant piece features a lyrical theme declaring his otherness from the norms of society. Like The Kinks' 'I'm Not Like Everybody Else' from four years earlier, 'Funny Ways' is a declaration of pride in individuality and difference, and there's a sense in which it's also a declaration of dedication to the Gentle Giant ethos over anything else in life, including personal and romantic relationships. Variations on this theme would turn up regularly over the years, and they give insight into the rather gnomic life of a musician and the personal price that's paid. The first section varies from delicate to staunch and could form the entire song, but instead, there's a rolling piano figure introduced at 2:02 that's the cue for a controlled, jazzy freak-out, finishing in a spectacular guitar solo from Gary and an array of *Sgt. Pepper's*-like military horn figures. Before, that is, it returns to the original theme with tuned percussion backing.

'Alucard' (Shulman, Shulman, Shulman, Minnear)

Introduced with a particularly grinding, lumbering riff polluted by a determinedly dirty synth and featuring organ, sax and trumpets, the first few minutes of 'Alucard' (Dracula backwards) are reminiscent of Van der Graaf Generator at their most nihilistic, and it's proof that even on their first album, Gentle Giant were masters of the swaggering groove. This is not the pastel stuff that progressive rock is often painted as by its detractors. 'Someone help me/terror fills my soul', goes one lyrical couplet although the vocals – processed as they are with a backwards-modified effect and vastly overdubbed – are used sparingly in what is essentially an instrumental track that shows many of the musical tics and techniques that defined the band later on used in a kind of larval stage.

There's also a secondary, rollicking but less invasive guitar-led section that shows the group's slight debt to King Crimson. If you put this track together on a playlist with KC's 'Catfood', the combination of heaviosity and virtuosity would make them comfortable bedfellows. 'Alucard' would not be the last time that Gentle Giant would draw its subject matter from history and legend, and appropriately, Kerry is already exploring counterpoint on this track.

'Isn't It Quiet And Cold' (Shulman, Shulman, Shulman, Minnear)

Steeped in the kind of cosy, drawing-room nostalgia that first entered the pop lexicon with The Beatles' 'When I'm 64', this lovely ballad – unlike the rather pat lyrics of that song or the overwrought strings of 'She's Leaving Home' – manages to strike just the right tone.

It's a musically nimble gem with an observational lyric about walking home late at night through suburbia, having missed the last bus, and it's gorgeous. Its dual violin (both bowed and pizzicato), cello, harpsichord and strummed acoustic guitar (not to mention the airy harmony background vocals or the short glockenspiel solo) are beautifully woven together into an elegant and charming concoction that somewhat anticipates the pop/orchestral experiment of Roy Wood and Jeff Lynne on the first Electric Light Orchestra album of a year later.

'Nothing At All' (Shulman, Shulman, Shulman, Minnear)
Like the previous track, the epic nine minutes and six seconds of 'Nothing At All' is quite untypical of later Gentle Giant, but stands on its own as a superb exposition of moody 1970 rock, and is indicative of the way certain influences were rubbing together at the time to forge new fusions.

The introductory acoustic guitar line is spookily similar to that of Led Zeppelin's 'Stairway To Heaven' of just a year later, while the lush harmony vocals are straight off The Beatles' *Abbey Road*, with perhaps a touch of the first Crosby, Still and Nash album. It's also disarmingly similar – especially the distinctive descending bass line – to parts of the Pretty Things' *Parachute*, which was recorded at Abbey Road Studios and released in June of 1970.

Which isn't to suggest that Gentle Giant were ever derivative, just that these things were 'in the air' that year. There are a number of factors that mark the song as distinctive, as well, because the band can never be accused of doing just one remarkable thing in a composition. Included in this list is one of their patented killer riffs, but the first time it comes around it's just a tease. Derek eventually gets into shouting mode while the big riff flagellates behind him and Gary Green somehow miraculously manages a dual lead guitar line.

And this is where it all gets ridiculous. Yes, it's the infamous phased drum solo. Word has it that it involved the various members of the group and that it was a lot of fun. And after all, percussion workouts were a real highlight of their live sets. But sorry, this three-and-a-half-minute drum solo seems to last an age and its overlay of piano noodling (with a touch of Liszt's 'Liebestraum No. 3' for good measure) not only plays out like a psychedelic relic but sadly destroys the mood built up by the piece. It's possible that being Zappa fans, they'd witnessed similar malarkey at The Mothers Of Invention's UK dates, but there's an essential difference: his music was built on satire, so there was no mood to break.

Based on a composition by Kerry Minnear, the song's lyrical theme harks back to 'Funny Ways', in that it's a critique of, 'This little girl who had everything/Finds she's nothing at all'. It's not explicitly stated, but the implication is that she's rejected the musician as too risky a

37

proposition, and therefore, it's her loss. Once again, it's a pointer towards the seemingly rather hermetic life of the group.

'Why Not?' (Shulman, Shulman, Shulman, Minnear)

The penultimate piece (and last music of any significance) on *Gentle Giant*, 'Why Not?' contains only trace elements of the group we know and love. After their percussion wig-out on 'Nothing At All', they pick up the reigns with a ballsy, almost Deep Purple-like organ-drenched, riff-heavy number that's one of the few times we get to hear Green take one of his florid, bluesy electric guitar solos. It's only a partial success and there's a bit of blues-boogie in here that might have come off as less clichéd in the celebratory atmosphere of a live concert.

But that's not all. Take note of the first, tantalizingly brief madrigal-influenced section (with recorders!) because we'll be getting much more of that over the next few albums. It's only a few bars and if the group had gone in a different direction than they did, this may have been simply a stylistic tic or brief digression. But we know better.

And Phil's words, which go against the grain to paint romantic love in bleak colours, also contain the DNA of the group's later lyrical themes; existential, and determined not to compromise.

'The Queen' (Shulman, Shulman, Shulman, Minnear)

It's only a fragment really, at a mere 1:26, but this is a fairly silly version of 'God Save The Queen' as reimagined for electric guitar. I guess they had their reasons.

Acquiring The Taste (1971)

Personnel:

Derek Shulman: lead and backing vocals, alto saxophone, clavichord, cowbell

Phil Shulman: clarinet, saxophone, trumpet, piano, claves, maracas, lead and backing vocals

Ray Shulman: bass, violin, guitar, tambourine, triangle, backing vocals

Kerry Minnear: Hammond organ, Minimoog, Mellotron, piano, harpsichord, electric piano, celeste, clavichord, tympani, xylophone, vibraphone, cello, maracas, tambourine, lead and backing vocals

Gary Green: guitar, mandolin, bass, voice

Martin Smith: drums, tambourine

Paul Cosh: trumpet, organ

Tony Visconti: recorders, percussion

Produced at Advision and A.I.R studios, January to April 1971 by Tony Visconti, engineered by Martin Rushent

Release date: July 16, 1971

Running time: 39:26

The group were reportedly bitter at the absence of any kind of buzz around their first album, and that's understandable. They had the cool label backing, the name producer and a strong debut. And all around them, their contemporaries were blossoming out of the undergrowth and onto the charts.

Happily, this commercial failure strengthened their resolve, where it might have broken a lesser band. You can feel the determination not only to succeed but to do so on their own terms, on Phil Shulman's liner notes for *Acquiring The Taste*, which was released a mere ten months after their debut:

It is our goal to expand the frontiers of contemporary music at the risk of being very unpopular. We have recorded each composition with the one thought – that it should be unique, adventurous and fascinating. It has taken every shred of our combined musical and technical knowledge to achieve this. From the outset, we have abandoned all preconceived thoughts of blatant commercialism. Instead, we hope to give you something far more substantial and fulfilling.

Rock writer Paul Stump (whose deeply flawed 2005 book on Gentle Giant took the title of this album) accused Phil's statement of 'self-regarding, pompous flummery', but it's a great insight on the group's convictions. And although it's imbued with a certain naivety, it also gels with the spirit of the time and – most importantly – honestly represents the adventurousness of *Acquiring The Taste*.

Unfortunately, the cover art of Gentle Giant's second album is more well known – and notorious – than the astonishing music on the vinyl. Preppy music website *Pitchfork* voted it one of the worst album covers of all time for its depiction of what appears to be an arse-licking tongue. In fact, when the gatefold is opened it's revealed to be a peach, but the allusion is clear: this was intended as a pointed critique of the avaricious commerciality of the record industry.

But let's get to the music, because *Acquiring The Taste* is the album on which Gentle Giant's interest in early music became overt, and it gave the group a sound so distinctive that – even amongst the furtive experimentation and musical virtuosity of other early 1970s progressive rock bands – would make them impossible to mistake for any other ensemble.

Back with Tony Visconti on production duties and with a capable and innovative young engineer in Martin Rushent (who would later become synonymous with post-punk groups like The Stranglers and The Human League), with *Acquiring The Taste*, Gentle Giant found a reliably great studio in Advision that they would subsequently return to for all their best work. And given that the first album was recorded quickly because it was already road-tested, this second album gave the group an opportunity to write and experiment in the studio.

It's here that the music of Gentle Giant is suddenly ripe with techniques like counterpoint and polyphony, poly-meters and metrical complexity. Kerry Minnear's studies at the Royal College Of Music and his abiding interest in early music seems to have spurred the Shulman brothers to adopt this musical architecture, although it's worth reiterating that this was not a purist attempt to update early music but instead, a bold initiative to create something entirely new via a fusion of styles both ancient and modern. The incredible dynamic of Gentle Giant was in the contrast between its component parts and its rock instrumentation. This wasn't dry academia nor simply 'rocking the classics', but a serious exploration of form in an attempt to write great compositions and perform them with power and precision.

But... the fact that *Acquiring The Taste* failed to make much more commercial impact than the first outing was perhaps an indication of a two-fold problem. As discussed in my introduction, England in the early

1970s seemed endeared of anything except its own history and musical traditions, which were pilloried throughout that decade to look Monty Pythonesque. In this atmosphere, how could a group seriously take on the stylistic characteristics of the middle ages and the Renaissance and expect any critical traction?

Adding to the problem, was the small fact that *Acquiring The Taste*, though it started brilliantly and contained many dazzling moments, failed to capitalise on those great moments on Side two of its journey.

'Pantagruel's Nativity' (Shulman, Shulman, Shulman, Minnear)

Inspired by *Gargantua And Pantagruel*, a satirical novel about the adventures of two (gentle) giants written by the French Renaissance writer Francois Rabelais, *Acquiring The Taste's* opening gambit comes on like something from the court of King Arthur... or at least, it reprises the medieval-era sound that we associate with the myth-encrusted fifth Century king. But in reality, it's a nifty composite of structural borrowings, and some of the classic flourishes here are probably drawn as much from the baroque stylings of the likes of Purcell than of his medieval antecedents. It pays not to care too much and just enjoy the wondrous melange, which on 'Pantagruel's Nativity' packs more detail and dynamic shifts into its six minutes and 50 seconds than many bands manage in a lifetime.

Beginning with a cute overdubbed Moog melody (Advision reputedly had a modular Moog setup that was six feet high), and then Kerry's choir-boy vocals, the piece slowly builds with some classic prog flourishes, including Mellotron billowing over strummed acoustic guitar, beautifully controlled electric guitar, plus flute and trumpet parts. Compared to the group's later work, it's all uncharacteristically glorious. It's precisely at the 2:12 mark that the real business of Gentle Giant begins, however, with a great walloping guitar riff and some counterpoint singing that sends shivers down the spine with its spooky dissonance. It's a singing style that has some similarities to the Bulgarian choral tradition which contrasts richly harmonic lines with the dissonance of microtones, but Gentle Giant combine this technique with multipart vocals that, when mixed with the killer guitar riff, provide either a real challenge or a fine stimulus for the senses – depending on your personal disposition.

What could happen from here? Why, there's then a vibraphone solo, over which the saxes graze, and a fairly conventional guitar solo from Gary, before that monster riff reappears along with the spooky vocals.

41

After some victorious-sounding parping on trumpet, there's a brief reprise for the pure-voiced Minnear.

'Pantagruel's Nativity' is one of the last times Gentle Giant will provide anything this prog-symphonic, and it won't be too long before it relegates the Mellotron to a bit-part player and tightens its rhythmic grid.

'Edge Of Twilight' (Shulman, Shulman, Shulman, Minnear)

It's again Kerry's ethereal vocals holding court on this quietly stunning piece, and it's mostly his work, including the orchestral percussion segment in which tympanis battle with xylophones. Despite its short duration (3:47) and seeming minimalism, 'Edge Of Twilight' is packed with minute detail. Listen, for instance, for the gorgeous reeds and strings, or the magical, sadly brief acoustic guitar and clavinet arpeggiations at 1:54.

Where some progressive rock bands could rightly be accused of excess, this wee gem is a great example of how that surplus of musical ideas and information could be so perfectly worked into the overall structure of a composition that it added exponentially to the overall work.

'The House, The Street, The Room' (Shulman, Shulman, Shulman, Minnear)

With its Phil Shulman lyric about 'the place you went to score your drugs', this song's opening piano-based melody is instantly reminiscent of the kind of playful cat and mouse/cops and robbers themes used on old films to achieve a mood that's suspended somewhere between spooky and comical. Derek's shouted vocal, however, is pure anguish ('my time is spent in chains and confusion'), while the contrasting angelic background harmonies bear a striking resemblance to those of early 10cc. And really, *Acquiring The Taste* is every bit the studio concoction those endlessly layered, smart and intricate 10cc records were, and just as unplayable in live performance.

It soon moves into a brief section featuring gently picked acoustic guitar and the voices of Kerry and Phil, and back and forth between the two contrasting moods before breaking off at 1:50 into a mercifully short improvisation between piano, xylophone and horns, and a powerful reiteration of the original theme and heavy organ-laced riffing with some serious guitar wrangling, before one more final breakdown of component elements.

The piece is even more complex than it sounds, with its main compositional thrust coming from Kerry, who has described it as an exercise in diminished sevenths. Gary has been quoted as saying: 'At one point, there are four different phrases going at the same time. They play repeatedly, cross and intermingle. Each time a phrase is played, it's performed on a different instrument... There are 32 instruments in total going around in a circle.'

As for the subject matter of the song, it's hard to imagine that the members of Gentle Giant ever did drugs in a serious way, given the rigour with which they worked and the intense discipline that must have been required.

'Acquiring The Taste' (Minnear)

One of the most interesting facets of Gentle Giant is the seemingly democratic way they worked, where each member did his bit to bring a composition to completion for the overall good of the band.

The album's title track is one of the few occasions in their eleven-album discography where one member hogs all the limelight, but it's a mere sliver of a song at 1:36. This was Kerry's chance to follow in the footsteps of Wendy Carlos' groundbreaking 1968 Moog record, *Switched On Bach*, and to do his modernised baroque thing on Advision's spectacular Moog setup. Rock fans may despair, but anyone who appreciates the virtual synthesis of instruments like the Moog – or Minnear's own compositional ability – will find some charm in this diversion.

'Wreck' (Shulman, Shulman, Shulman, Minnear)

An updating of the sea shanty tradition, 'Wreck' tells the story of the horrific drowning of a fishing boat's crew. Inspired by Byron's *Don Juan*, it's one of the weaker tracks on *Acquiring The Taste*, with a lyric that pointlessly dwells on the meaninglessness of their deaths and a 'hey-hey-yeah-yeah' chorus that's on the edge of irritating due to its repetition.

There is some relief from the Derek-led choruses with short vocal sections featuring Phil and Kerry, and the main theme even breaks off for a very brief section of recorder malarkey, but the best part of half a century on and 'Wreck' still sounds like one of Gentle Giant's weaker ideas.

'The Moon Is Down' (Shulman, Shulman, Shulman, Minnear)

Its opening few bars of multiple saxes gives 'The Moon Is Down' a chamber-jazz feel before the addition of harpsichord and Derek's vocals, which are soon joined in a spectacular harmony vocal section which is again not unlike the intricate, sophisticated work 10cc were doing in the studio around the same time. Then it fires up into a short, overtly jazz-flecked section with horns and delightfully pizzicato guitar and moist, pleasantly burbling organ before a tailpiece that returns to the original vocal theme. Phew!

If there's a problem here, it's that it feels a little as if too many sections have been grafted onto each other, and the vocal melody is just a bit too much like a shadow of the sea shanty that preceded it. Having said that, it's a rewarding job to pick apart its constituent elements, and while it never congeals into a Gentle Giant classic, there's much to enjoy here.

'Black Cat' (Shulman, Shulman, Shulman, Minnear)

The same could be said for 'Black Cat', with its memorable opening violin melody, which is echoed in pizzicato, and its slightly spooky, rather slinky groove. With a lead vocal by Phil, this is a minor entry in the Gentle Giant discography – in the same way that 'Cat Food' is a minor song in King Crimson's discography – but it's musically very cool and wonderful on its own terms, and again, the studio experimentation makes it a vivid string-laden delight.

'Black Cat' is different than the preceding cut in that it sustains its mood beautifully and has a lucid, almost film-like quality that begs the question: why the heck didn't they earn some handy cash by doing film soundtrack work?

'Plain Truth' (Shulman, Shulman, Shulman, Minnear)

The longest song on *Acquiring The Taste* at seven minutes and 36 seconds, 'Plain Truth' is influenced by the nihilistic philosophy of Albert Camus and seems to be taking a potshot at religion and anyone who contends that there's more to life than the physical reality in which we find ourselves trapped. 'Plain truth means nothing/Cry, laugh and cry again/You question answers/Born, live and die, Amen', sings Derek on this strident piece. *The Plain Truth* was, in fact, a widely circulated and free-of-charge evangelical publication, which probably would wend its way into the Shulman brothers' parents' letterbox when they were children.

Beginning with an electric wah-wah violin in the left channel and someone ordering Wimpy hamburgers and fries in the other, it's a powerful, almost anthemic, piece that would have made for a gratifying live experience. Interestingly, the groovy guitar/bass figure that laces its way through the piece is more than a little like a section of Mike Oldfield's runaway smash hit of two years later, *Tubular Bells*. They would have been justifiably resentful at his success while they thrashed around in the margins, knowing that their music was equally deserving but never quite getting the breaks.

Three Friends (1972)
Personnel:
Derek Shulman: lead and backing vocals
Phil Shulman: saxophone, lead and backing vocals
Ray Shulman: bass, violin, guitar, backing vocals
Kerry Minnear: Hammond organ, Minimoog, Mellotron, piano, electric piano, harpsichord, clavinet, vibraphone, percussion, lead and backing vocals
Gary Green: guitar, mandolin
Malcolm Mortimore: drums
Produced at Advision and Command studios, December 1971 by Gentle Giant, engineered by Martin Rushent
Release date: April 14, 1972
Running time: 35:24

The continued lack of palpable success or critical acclaim might, once again, have finished a lesser band, but Gentle Giant was back in the studio to record their third album just eight months after the release of *Acquiring The Taste*. Changes were afoot, however. Gone was long-serving drummer Martin Smith, who had survived the dissolution of Simon Dupree And The Big Sound, only to be deemed not fit for service after the first two Gentle Giant albums. The group was searching for someone with more muscle, but they wouldn't find quite what they wanted with the inexperienced Malcolm Mortimer, who lasted little longer than it took to record their third album. Gone too, was producer Tony Visconti, although they kept the services of engineer Martin Rushent, with whom they had a friendly and productive creative relationship. Initial recordings were made in Command Studios but – confused by the alien environment – they soon returned to the familiar surrounds of Advision. Still, it's obvious in listening to *Three Friends* that the group were grappling with the demands of self-production as well as integrating a new drummer.

Having an overall concept for the album (a first for Gentle Giant) will have simplified the writing process, but the result – both compositionally and conceptually – doesn't live up to the expectations set by *Acquiring The Taste*. On its own terms, *Three Friends* has its charms, but when laid out next to the heavy hitters in this exceptional year for progressive rock (think Yes's all-time classic *Close To The Edge*, Emerson, Lake and Palmer's brilliant, studio-crafted *Trilogy* or Gentle Giant's occasional road buddies Jethro Tull's *Thick As A Brick*) it's easy to see why it hardly made an impression.

It doesn't help that the concept about three school buddies growing up, growing apart and diverging down different paths in life, is a little simplistic, and the result reminds this author of that classic Woody Allen line in *Annie Hall*:

Right now it's only a notion, but I think I can get money to make it into a concept, and later turn it into an idea.

That might sound harsh, but the whole concept (which Phil said was 'about what really happens to people as they grow older') could have been reduced down to one song. And while the record continues the stylistic roads furrowed on *Acquiring The Taste*, there's little of the overt experimentation or the dissonance and darkness that gave the group its balance and prevented it from accusations of tweeness. Instead, it's even a little sentimental, in parts.

It's worth pointing out, however, that the characteristics that would dominate Gentle Giant on its best albums (*Octopus, In A Glass House, The Power And The Glory*) were already poking their wee buds through the foliage. In many ways, *Three Friends* sounds like a step backwards as the group grapples with the challenges of self-production and a blues influence that would never be overt again, but on songs like 'Mister Class And Quality' we can already hear the complex, circular interplay that somewhat characterises the group later on, beginning to take shape, and which defines them as the perfect ensemble organism.

'Prologue' (Shulman, Shulman, Shulman, Minnear)
The album starts well with this perky piece featuring piano, guitar and squelchy synthesiser, and its lyrics rendered in what by now is a Gentle Giant trademark: the multi-part counterpoint vocals. As with so many Gentle Giant songs, the six minutes and fourteen seconds of 'Prologue' has more packed into its running length than many whole albums by other bands.

'Schooldays' (Shulman, Shulman, Shulman, Minnear)
The album's longest track at 7:37, this is a piece about boys who think they'll be friends forever, but for whom doubts are starting to creep into play. One of the highlights of *Three Friends*, 'Schooldays' features jazzy guitar and vibraphone on the intro and outro, and more counterpoint singing.

The genius idea here, however, was using a boy soprano (actually Phil's son) to express the first flicker of doubt about the future of the three boys, and the purity and naivety of the vocal, together with the ominous chords fading into drifting Mellotron and piano, evoke the feeling of lingering doubt on the edge of their cosy world. Being very much a studio creation, there's quite a bit of jiggery-pokery in terms of stereo presentation. A good example of this the line:

When we were to... (right channel) ...gether (left channel).

So, not only do we have the head-spinning impact of counterpoint but the two syllables of a single word being flung around dimensionally from speaker to speaker.

'Working All Day' (Shulman, Shulman, Shulman, Minnear)
It's probably apt that a song about the three boys having grown up and become slaves to their jobs has a workmanlike feel, but this strident piece – and specifically Derek's vocal lines, which evoke the annoying repetition of 'Wreck', the sea shanty from *Acquiring The Taste* – is notable mostly for the interesting studio manipulation of its honking horns, and it's organ solo.

'Peel The Paint' (Shulman, Shulman, Shulman, Minnear)
For 'Peel The Paint', Kerry wrote a Vivaldi-like violin part that required Ray to multitrack his instrument into a veritable string section. It's an impressive feat, but unfortunately sounds grafted on in much the same way as the orchestral sections of Yes's failed experiments on *Time And A Word*. But what saves the track and transforms it into something else altogether, is the subsequent great big bluesy riff, which gives Gary the rare opportunity for a gratuitous bit of guitar mangling.
It's a song about how 'nice' people can explode into monsters, and the music attempts to explode out of its faux-baroque beginnings into a mad riff monster. While it's flawed, it's also next to impossible for the listener not to enjoy and appreciate its audacious spirit.

'Mister Class And Quality' (Shulman, Shulman, Shulman, Minnear)
The album's possible high watermark, which is again originated by Kerry. This piece is a chrysalis version of what Gentle Giant would become on what would be their peak years of 1973-1975: there's the

three-part counterpoint singing (of course) but also a cool groove over which Gary and Kerry play a gloriously tight-arsed circular latticework of notes.

Lyrically, it's about the friend for whom material riches had become the one focus and his tunnel vision that his way is the right way.

'Three Friends' (Shulman, Shulman, Shulman, Minnear)
The title track and last song segues from 'Mister Class And Quality', and they go so well together that it's hard to imagine them prised apart. 'Three Friends' is one of Gentle Giant's most overtly prog-symphonic pieces, and it makes great use of the Mellotron, and the thrilling massed voices that overdubbing had made possible to achieve.

And of course, it brings the story to a conclusion by rueing what the three friends had lost over the years.

Octopus (1972)

Personnel:

Derek Shulman: lead and backing vocals, saxophone

Phil Shulman: saxophone, trumpet, mellophone, lead and backing vocals

Ray Shulman: bass, violin, viola, guitar, percussion, backing vocals

Kerry Minnear: Hammond organ, Minimoog, Mellotron, piano, electric piano, regal, harpsichord, Clavinet, vibraphone, cello, percussion, lead and backing vocals

Gary Green: electric guitar, percussion

John Weathers: drums, percussion, xylophone

Produced at Advision and Command studios, July 24 to August 5, 1972, by Gentle Giant, engineered by Martin Rushent

Release date: December 1, 1972

Running time: 34:09

After the slight disappointment of *Three Friends*, the next chapter in the Gentle Giant story gave fans all the justification they needed for having stuck with the group thus far.

Dropped on an unsuspecting public at the end of 1972, *Octopus* was, and is, an incredible record and enduring fan favourite. It's been sampled by hip-hop groups and has recently started popping up on magazine lists of best progressive rock albums, although at the time, once again, its impact on the market was slight: making it only to number 170 on the *Billboard* charts hardly does this crowning classic any justice.

Octopus played to all of Gentle Giant's strengths while expunging anything that wasn't core to the group's values, and the great facilitator was new drummer John 'Pugwash' Weathers, a seasoned musician who made it easy for them to do their tricky metrical changes over his solid, powerful beat. Heck, at times he even makes them swing!

Mortimore just hadn't worked out, and a motorcycle accident that put him out of action for months must have seemed like the perfect time to end his tenure. After all, Gentle Giant had a relentless touring and recording schedule to maintain, and Weathers – who had played with Graham Bond's Magick, Pete Brown And Piblokto, the Grease Band and Man – could pick up his sticks and go.

Deriving its title from the album's pet name, 'octo-opus' (it has eight tracks), *Octopus* is a record on which each individual works together as part of a greater organism; a defining feature of Gentle Giant at its best. While the compositions mainly fall to Kerry and Ray (and the lyrics to Derek and Phil), the performances mesh perfectly and, shorn of any typical progressive rock grandstanding or long soloing, the playing is a characterful servant of the song.

It's interesting to note that the longest song on *Octopus* is a mere 5:53, and that most sit around the four-minute mark, in direct contrast to the typically gargantuan running time and epic grandeur of the era. The short running time, however, does not denote any concession-making, and within each song, there's a world of complexity.

If there's any one member whose work stands out above all others, it's Kerry, whose writing is crammed with incredible detail ('statistical density', as Frank Zappa once remarked about his own music) and articulates itself with great alacrity. It's not until you really analyse Gentle Giant's music that you start to understand Kerry's particular writing and performative genius. While his music is densely packed with notes that must have been difficult to render in a group context, there's none of the showboating of a Rick Wakeman or Keith Emerson. In fact, his writing often defers to the group ethos, and it's the way his keyboards fit into the greater instrumental schema that matters.

In the UK, the album featured a cover by Roger Dean who was riding high at the time with his Yes cover artwork. It's far from his best work (compare its simple painting of an octopus with the branding brilliance of his Yes covers or the distinctive visual aroma of *Demons and Wizards* for Uriah Heep the same year). Maybe that's why the American record company opted to commission their own cover from Charles E. White III, who turns out not to be the African/American artist that Wikipedia links to, but the painter of dozens of album covers in the '70s and '80s, including JJ Cale's *Troubadour*, Cheech& Chong's *Up In Smoke* and the London Symphony Orchestra's rendition of The Who's *Tommy*. His airbrushed octopus in a jar felt all wrong to UK fans but has remained the image of choice for American fans to this day.

'The Advent Of Panurge' (Shulman, Shulman, Shulman, Minnear)
Which Gentle Giant track would you play for someone who had never heard the group but was expressing curiosity? 'The Advent Of Panurge' must be one of the top contenders. A genuine classic that was included as part of a medley in their live show right up to the end, it's a song that's chock-full of just about everything that makes Gentle Giant distinctive and exceptional.

While the group move away from the conceptual conceit of *Three Friends*, *Octopus* has a kind of lyrical conceptual continuity (to abuse another Zappa term) in that the words penned by Phil and Ray are often bleakly existential and inspired by literature. 'The Advent Of Panurge' (like 'Pantagruel's Nativity' on *Acquiring The Taste*) was inspired by 16th-century French author Francois Rabelais and his five satirical *Gargantua* and *Pantagruel* novels and is sung partly in madrigal-style by Kerry and Phil, while as always, Derek's stronger voice takes the declamatory sections. Part of its spine-tingling delight is derived from the contrast between the delicate sections that sound like they come from a time of ancient myth, and the ballsy rock sections that – blessed with Weathers' powerful drumming – add an irrepressible sense of swing to proceedings. When Gentle Giant 'rock out', of course, it's quite unlike any other group, and the sheer musicality throughout the four minutes and forty-three seconds of this classic track gives it enough ballast to ensure the listener will still be uncovering new layers in the composition and instrumentation after repeated exposure.

'Raconteur Troubadour' (Shulman, Shulman, Shulman, Minnear)
Here the group plays up the early music aspect by having Derek take on the character of a medieval minstrel, and the largely acoustic (apart from electric bass and piano) 'Raconteur Troubadour' consists of a fascinating mix of styles.

There's an earthy folksiness with its tambourine and catgut fiddle, but the middle section with its classically derived piano shows that Gentle Giant were more interested in impact, surprise and the resultant surrealism than being 'authentic'.

The song is brought to what suggests an imminent conclusion with a violin-led baroque-styled denouement that's purely symphonic but swings back to a catapulting beat and some more folksy revelry.

'A Cry For Everyone' (Shulman, Shulman, Shulman, Minnear)
With possibly the most depressing lyrics in the entire Gentle Giant canon, 'A Cry For Everyone' (written by Ray) is based on the books of French philosopher/author Albert Camus, whose contention was that human life was essentially worthless.

Run, why should I run away/When at the end the only truth certain/One day everyone dies/If only to justify life.

Derek sings at the start of the track over a fairly standard boogie rock guitar sound, before the group gets into one of the tight circular grooves that were becoming a Gentle Giant trademark, and includes a really nasty synth solo which is of course – given the brevity of the track – vastly abbreviated.

While hardly a highlight, the song shows that the group was adventurous both musically and philosophically. Its somewhat bleak subject matter would have better fit the nihilism of the punk or grunge era, perhaps.

'Knots' (Shulman, Shulman, Shulman, Minnear)

Like 'The Advent Of Panurge', 'Knots' would become one of the group's enduring classics and was to be incorporated into a 'best of' medley that never failed to 'wow' the punters in concert, and like that song, it contains a vast trove of the group's secret musical herbs and spices.

Featuring the single most impactful expression of the group's counterpoint singing smarts, the vocal four-part vocal arrangement was madrigal-inspired and utilised the words of Scottish psychiatrist/author RD Laing, whose work fit the zeitgeist of the early 1970s. Laing's words are about the habits and patterns that limit human potential, a subject that must have been close to the heart of this most adventurous of groups.

There's inspired use of xylophone, processed violin and sax before the piece breaks out into a brief but victorious jaunt (symbolic of the way we occasionally break out of our life patterns?) and, eventually, a stinging, almost demonic riff. One of the all-time most exciting vocal performances on record, 'Knots' is a piece that constantly teases us with short bursts of riff-ology before it darts back to some more xylophone malarkey. Simply extraordinary.

'The Boys In The Band' (Shulman, Shulman, Shulman, Minnear)

Laughter, and then a stereophonic coin spinning.

A rare undertaking for Gentle Giant, 'The Boys In The Band' is an instrumental workout that showcases their musical chops, but without any of the individual ego-stroking so typical of progressive rock bands. This is a display of collective virtuosity starting out with a vigorous, sax-led jazz-rock theme that sounds like a dead-ringer for Frank Zappa's George Duke-era ensembles, then transitions seamlessly into a reflective section with cute-sounding baby-organ, before smashing back into the super-fast, muscular head.

But wait, there's more. There's always more. In fact, the song actually finishes with a partly reflective section containing some beautiful guitar and synth soloing over composed horn lines. Except that the main theme is back to getcha one more time, and then fade-out!

'Dog's Life' (Shulman, Shulman, Shulman, Minnear)
Contrasts are rife on *Octopus*, and this rather gorgeous, tongue-in-cheek ballad masquerading as a song about man's best friend, is actually a tribute to the band's roadies. There's a rather doleful vibe to this song, sung by Phil, with its dainty strings contrasting with comedic synth and sax sounds.
Another minor gem.

'Think Of Me With Kindness' (Shulman, Shulman, Shulman, Minnear)
It does seem a strange programming quirk that two ballads are sequenced side by side, but this one has a much more hand-on-heart flavour than 'Dog's Life'.
Kerry sings this intimate and oddly effecting piece, which he keeps disarmingly simple (by Gentle Giant standards). It's an old-fashioned ballad with a classical grandness that uses swelling instrumentation in a manner not unlike some of the group's contemporaries – Genesis, for instance.

'River' (Shulman, Shulman, Shulman, Minnear)
The firm pulse (and swing) of Weathers' drums is evident on 'River', the last time that Phil and Derek sing together on record. Like all Gentle Giant pieces, it could be claimed that 'River' isn't just one song, but a series of micro-melodies and riffs with a few unifying themes. It certainly goes through its changes, and there's just enough time for a bit of an end-of-album jam featuring a decent Gary guitar solo, but nothing too long or extravagant.
With its distinctive electric violin, warm organ sound, and some studio jiggery-pokery in the stereophonic whizzing around of sounds and layers, it's an apt way to end the album and an era.

In A Glass House (1973)

Personnel:
Derek Shulman: lead and backing vocals, saxophone, recorder
Ray Shulman: bass, violin, guitar, percussion, backing vocals
Kerry Minnear: Hammond organ, Moog synthesizer, Mellotron, piano,
electric piano, harpsichord, clavinet, vibraphone, glockenspiel, marimba,
timpani, cello, percussion, lead and backing vocals
Gary Green: acoustic guitar, electric guitar, percussion
John Weathers: drums, percussion
Produced at Advision, July 1973 by Gentle Giant and Gary Martin,
engineered by Gary Martin
Release date: September 21, 1973
Running time: 38:08

Within a two-year timeframe, Gentle Giant had weathered the
departure of drummer Martin Smith, the unsuccessful deployment
of Malcolm Mortimore, and the introduction of John Weathers to the
group. And now, another seismic shift: Phil Shulman opted to leave so
that he could dedicate his time to his wife and young children. One of
the key components of Gentle Giant, the member largely responsible
for the group's lyric ideas and one of the integral three Shulman
brothers, was gone.

The remaining members chose to push on, but the resultant album
reflected the struggle of adapting to life after Phil. Fans are still divided
about *In A Glass House* after all this time, some citing it as a firm
favourite and a bold new direction, while others see it as merely a
jumping stone towards the indisputably great *The Power And The Glory*
(1974). It must have been galling that despite its brilliance, *Octopus*
had failed to achieve the commercial rewards it so richly deserved. So,
where to go next?

There's nothing quite as ornate as 'Knots' or 'The Advent Of Panurge'
on *In A Glass House*, but it makes up for that by turning up the volume
and adding the kind of rock firepower that the group exhibited in
concert. Not that it exactly mirrored the live experience of Gentle Giant
– those unlucky enough not to have the chance to catch the ensemble
in the flesh would have to wait until the 1977 release of *Playing The
Fool* for a taste of that – but there was more muscle on its bones and
more emphasis on electric instruments.

Despite its fraught circumstances, *In A Glass House* is an astonishing
piece of work and it seems less a time-capsule of the early '70s than its

predecessors due to the undeniably powerful thrust of its rock moves and the slightly austere, moody nature of the songs and music, which casts it into the same timeless cauldron as contemporaneous King Crimson and Van der Graaf Generator. Like all Gentle Giant work, it demands repeat exposure, because it can seem somehow forbidding on first taste.

In a move that can only be described as idiotic, the group's American record company, Columbia, rejected the album as uncommercial, which meant that despite heavy touring in America and virtually no profile in the UK, *In A Glass House* would only be available in the US as an expensive import. Ironically, US fans went nuts for the record, and it was easily the group's best-selling title there up to that point. It certainly featured the most eye-catching cover artwork of any Gentle Giant release: the 'picture' was a cellophane 'window' behind which were lithographs of the boys in the band. Nineteen seventy-three was a year of over-the-the top packaging. Following on from the fake newspaper adorning Jethro Tull's *Thick As A Brick* the previous year, '73 saw the extravagant multiple fold-out HR Giger artwork of ELP's *Brain Salad Surgery* and more like it. This must have been an expensive job, but one that certainly enticed many teenage progressive rock fans to invest.

Though not obviously conceptual, *In A Glass House* is roughly based around the aphorism, 'those who live in glass houses shouldn't throw stones', and the tracks do explore that concept in an elliptical way. The songs themselves are notably longer than those on *Octopus*, but they still sensibly stay within the ten-minute mark.

'The Runaway' (Shulman, Shulman, Minnear)
In A Glass House has one of the most distinctive openings (and closings) of any 1970s album: the sound of shattering glass, looped and repeated. It's a novelty that somewhat wears off, but it's emblematic of 1973, the year of sound effects (think Pink Floyd's *Dark Side Of The Moon*), and ties in loosely with the album's title.

'The Runaway' gets off to a brisk start, with a tale about an escaped convict, and his experience on the run, both actual and psychological. The music fades in over the looped glass effect with a trebly Clavinet-based theme and subtle guitar pickings that, as so often on this album, are a little Fripp-like. Immediately, we're aware of how well integrated everything is. There's a new confidence that allows the powerful riffing of the rock sections, Derek's vocal parts (often in a minor key just to create a sense of unease) and the various other eddies and tides of the composition to flow as one, with little sense of the fragmentary awkwardness that occasionally hampered their earlier work.

At 7:24, it's one of several songs on which the group allow themselves more time than usual to explore and restate themes. There are billowing clouds of vocals and cascading marimbas, but all the while there's a solid foundational groove where the physicality of the rhythm section is highlighted.

Eventually, Kerry enters with one of his troubadour vocals and recorders, but his section is only allowed so much oxygen before the declamatory guitar riffs reappear, then some circular melodic guitar-wizardry from Gary, followed by an unexpected, juicy marimba solo and overdubbed keyboards of various kinds.

'An Inmate's Lullaby' (Shulman, Shulman, Minnear)
And now, for something completely different. 'An Inmate's Lullaby' is a gorgeous wee ballad based on reverberating vibraphone and the deep boings of tympani. Derek's vocals are uncharacteristically mellow (sometimes processed through what sounds like a close-up megaphone effect), as he plays the part of an insane asylum inmate who is clearly disturbed. It's a charming lullaby with a dark centre and the kind of detour only a group as adept as Gentle Giant could successfully accomplish, and it provides welcome pause between the assertive rock gravitas of the songs that sandwich it.

'Way Of Life' (Shulman, Shulman, Minnear)
From the opening shout of 'Go!' you know that 'Way Of Life' means business. This is a full-throttle exposition of Gentle Giant at this juncture: drums and bass are up in the mix, with an unresolved Robert Fripp-style guitar arpeggiation followed by some squiggly synthesiser and even a bit of 'rocking out'.

Like 'Funny Ways' before it, 'Way Of Life' is an assertion of the right to have a life that's different than common folk. It's possible that Phil's decision to forgo the band ethos and the collective goals of life in a group for a normal family life, was something that provoked thought, and in the 7:52 of 'Way Of Life,' Derek seeks to examine the response of a female partner to his chosen way of life.

There can't have been much room for a conventional family life in the Gentle Giant 'boys in the band' ethos, and committing to a group that necessitated round the clock involvement, incessant touring and recording with little to show for it all financially, must have taken an incredible amount of conviction. It's a brilliant piece with one of Kerry's rock-symphonic sections towards the end, which suggests, musically, that the band credo had been triumphant, as it would be for the next seven years.

Finally, the piece winds up with some long, drawn-out, spooky organ notes. Perhaps this represents the doubt that lingers about whether this way of life was, in fact, the right decision, and that the way ahead isn't clear.

'Experience' (Shulman, Shulman, Minnear)

Almost as long (at 7:50) is 'Experience', which contrasts Kerry's lighter voice – sung in medieval style – with an immediate sense of building rock action. The piece quickly goes into a busy circular groove with an odd metre, which evolves with electric violin and organ. Then it all comes to a stop for some angelic 'sacred' voices (and what sounds like pump organ) and a simple bass figure, before the riffing swings back into action with an irrepressible groove.

This is the cue for Derek's declamatory vocal, the song telling the story of how his view of the world as a young man had consequences he was blinkered to, and that as a grown-up he's got a 'bond of duty' to others that his dawning consciousness now understands. The subject matter alludes to that of *Three Boys* and also the concept of *The Power And The Glory*.

Like so many of Gentle Giant's songs, 'Experience' is a musical puzzle to be consumed over multiple sessions and unlocked, piece-by-piece.

'A Reunion' (Shulman, Shulman, Minnear)

Another of Kerry's delightful ballads, 'A Reunion' is a nostalgic view of a past relationship that in a better world could have been Gentle Giant's 'In The Beginning': a crossover hit that wouldn't have alerted the unsuspecting to the band's usual, more confrontational and difficult material. With its restful and elegant multi-tracked parlour violins and gently picked acoustic guitar (and its brevity at only 2:11) once again it's a great pause before the grand finale that follows.

'In A Glass House' (Shulman, Shulman, Minnear)

The title track is a masterful conclusion to a great (and under-appreciated) album, with its numerous musical changes in time and tone that somehow manage to coalesce into an impressive overall experience. It's both an echo of everything that came before it and a great (and explosive) conclusion, with assertive rock sections, over which Derek sings, and some wonderful relief in brief, quiet sections.

Gary's guitar skills seem to improve with every album as he hones his style – carved in blues but now far from where he started and intensely disciplined – to suit whichever passage he's playing, whether it's the heaviosity of the riff-based sections or nimble acoustic fretwork on the quieter passages. The whole thing comes to a messy end with another outburst of breaking glass, followed by miniature samples from across the tracks, ending in psychedelic echoes.

The Power And The Glory (1974)

Personnel:
Derek Shulman: lead and backing vocals, saxophone,
Ray Shulman: bass, violin, guitar, vocals
Kerry Minnear: Hammond organ, Minimoog synthesizer, Mellotron, piano,
electric piano, clavinet, vibraphone, marimba, cello, percussion, lead and
backing vocals
Gary Green: acoustic guitar, electric guitar, vocals
John Weathers: drums, percussion
Produced at Advision, December 1973 to January 1974 by Gentle Giant,
engineered by Gary Martin
Release date: September 22, 1973
Running time: 37:11

As great as it was, *In A Glass House* was the product of a time of great
change in the band, and to some degree, its edginess reflected the
struggles the band were facing during its creation. *The Power And The
Glory*, however, finds Gentle Giant feeling confident and relaxed. The
lineup has settled, and they're able to play to all their strengths on a
record that many fans consider their best.

1974 was an odd year for progressive rock. Its most popular
exponents had peaked in '72 and '73, and it seemed there was nowhere
to go except to tumble into the absurdity of triple live albums and
egocentric solo albums. Gentle Giant, however, having never attained
the popularity that would have seen them perform to American arenas
full of youths stoned on downers, had consolidated into a mean and
lean lit firework of a band. The muscularity developed on *In A Glass
House* is once again used to great effect, but this time on songs that
sound disciplined, less fanciful and – without any detectable sign of
compromise – more accessible than any of their previous albums.

After the US record company's botched non-release of *In A Glass
House* and its unexpected success as an import, it sounds like they're
ready for another bout in the ring. And yes, *The Power And The Glory*
did chart there. It may have managed only a modest #78 on the
Billboard charts, but compared to the group's almost total invisibility
in their own country, it must have been a great encouragement. That
rating was no doubt helped by Gentle Giant's first US tour in a year-and-
a-half to support the album.

With its rather obvious but worthy concept about the corrupting
influence of power and power's ability to corrupt completely, *The*

Power And The Glory was a great excuse to combine some of their most powerful rock moves with an utterly cohesive evolution of all of the group's notable characteristics.

It's clear from the get-go that with *The Power And The Glory*, Gentle Giant have reached some kind of pinnacle. While it's not as gloriously experimental as *Acquiring The Taste* or as audaciously adventurous as *Octopus* or as edgy as *In A Glass House*, it's close to the perfect exposition of the group as a recording and performing unit. It's also proof that through sheer doggedness, the group could find a way to cut to the core of their sound and simplify it for easier public accessibility but without the usual attendant compromise. Not that the album doesn't contain some mindboggling complexity; it's just that there are fewer of these passages than on previous albums, and as a whole, what comes across is the sense of a band performing in real time.

And to tie in with the theme, the cover art featured an adaptation of a genuine vintage playing card, and the original cover featured distinctive rounded edges.

'Proclamation' (Shulman, Shulman, Minnear)

One of the most instantly unforgettable Gentle Giant songs, 'Proclamation' pins the album's theme to the village wall. Starting with sampled crowd sounds (a motif repeated sporadically throughout the song) and electric piano, its lyrics promote the idea of power used responsibly as being a good and necessary mechanism.

It's not long before we get into the busy repeated motifs that are such a feature of Gentle Giant, and particularly this album. Generally, these sequences (performed on whichever instruments take the group's fancy) will run for either three or four bars; a clever mechanism that gives the listener the chance to absorb and enjoy the sequence through repetition, before shuffling off in a different direction. In this instance, after the echoed, drawn-out exclamation of 'Hail!' there's a nifty guitar/ electric piano sequence with overlaid organ melody, followed by a more rocking groove, and then a short section that deserves an essay in its own right.

Suddenly, things go nuts, with some particularly throaty organ, followed by what sounds like one of Conlon Nancarrow's too-fast-for-human-hands player piano compositions, under which Ray's bass authoritatively guides the wayward ship. This builds up spectacularly to an overdubbed male choir (the band, of course!) singing, 'Hail to power and glory's way!' It's genuinely spooky, as the minor key riffs

underpinning the massed vocals hint at evil doings and the corruption
lurking around the edges of any powerful kingdom/government. Gary's
electric guitar does exactly what it needs to do while Ray's bass doubles
Gary's lines way down deep.

Amazingly, we're only just over four minutes into the composition's
6:47 running time when it takes a left turn and grounds to a halt, before
Kerry's electric piano and harpsichord slowly build up an almost funky
groove, the cue for a return to the original vocal theme, the crowd
sounds and a slow fade.

'So Sincere' (Shulman, Shulman, Minnear)
Unusually for Gentle Giant, 'So Sincere' uses irony to take a potshot
at a politician's insincerity, on a piece that's at once minimalist and
musically clever. Beginning with dual lines on sax and violin, and
then moving to a playful stop-start sequence over which Kerry sings
the lead, things quickly go intentionally askew with a circus jumble
of instrumentation and Derek repeating the intentionally broken-up
words: 'So! Sin! Cere!'

After that, the piece continues with a descending sequence and Kerry's
double-tracked, stereo vocal, before Derek comes back from another
rejoinder/reminder, and the tune blossoms out into a groove that gives
just enough breathing space for a luscious, tantalisingly brief guitar solo
by Gary before the sequence repeats once again. Just wonderful.

'Aspirations' (Shulman, Shulman, Minnear)
Had 'Aspirations' somehow been a hit, there's a chance that it could
have derailed the group in the same way as the saccharine AOR of
Chicago's 'If You Leave Me Now' did that group's wayward rock/jazz
fusion. Kerry had a real knack for writing achingly gorgeous ballads, but
thankfully, they were just too subtle and multi-layered to make chart-
fodder, and instead, their appearance on Gentle Giant albums always
gives the listener a chance to take a breather.

They may have served that purpose, but a song like 'Aspirations'
is a great piece in its own right, with a haunting vocal cadence, and
expressing as it does the hope that comes with every new government
that things will change for the better and that the people will get a new
deal that makes life fairer and easier.

All coming true, it depends on you... our times they are troubled times.
Tell us the way...

Built on mellow electric piano, with some gently strummed semi-acoustic guitar, Kerry's vocal lines are sung in a way that may specifically reference medieval styles but are also reminiscent of other inimitably English singers like Robert Wyatt, and Caravan's Pye Hastings and Richard Sinclair. This haunting song is Gentle Giant at its most direct and accessible.

'Playing The Game' (Shulman, Shulman, Minnear)
The second-to-longest song on *The Power And The Glory* at 6:45, 'Playing The Game' features one of the most niggling wee melodic sequences the group ever wrote, and coasts along on a sound that's inching a bit closer to the FM-rock style they were to adopt in their latter years.

This is a song of public confidence as the king announces that he's on top of the world and whatever he does will be the right decision for his people, and the style of the piece reflects that. He's allowed just a moment's doubt – voiced by Kerry – in an acknowledgement that he has unspoken thoughts inside his head. But mostly it's a track brimming with confidence, with some nice dirty bass (and some bass-as-guitar moments that shows the enduring influence of Jack Bruce) and mallets being struck throughout. There are twinkling electric piano and thematic guitar interjections, and many other elements are thrown into the mix, but everything is thought-through, none of which muddies the pot. It's the kind of piece you could almost imagine audience members gyrating to, especially the near-funky groove with its fruity organ solo. Yowza!

'Cogs In Cogs' (Shulman, Shulman, Minnear)
It's only just over three minutes in length, but 'Cogs In Cogs' really cooks. Featuring one of the busiest of the group's patented circular sequences, the piece features a strident vocal from Derek and the music's industrious nature is reflected in the theme, in which societal change is being bogged down in red tape:

All words saying nothing/The air is sour with discontent.

The song ably expresses the onward march of the industrial complex (whether set in early times or contemporary) and how nothing ever really changes – that we remain trapped in this infernal cycle of trusting in our leaders, who always let us down.

There's a brief snippet of simplified counterpoint and a cute synth theme before a return to the chorus of this most recognisable of Gentle Giant pieces. In one interview, Gary explained it thus:

> The first part is in 6/4, the second 15/8, meaning the two melodies line up differently in 6 different ways: the phrases meet every 60 semiquavers.

If you say so.

'No God's A Man' (Shulman, Shulman, Minnear)
A sterling example of just how under-sung Gentle Giant are, is the first minute of this track, which is a self-contained, haunting and beguiling low-key instrumental section featuring acoustic guitar and marimba that could almost have come from Frank Zappa's *Lumpy Gravy*, or some moody early '70s film composer. The fact that it then changes gear and features Derek leading a counterpoint vocal means that, inevitably, the quieter section is seldom acknowledged.

In fact, while many of Gentle Giant's most exciting moments are the complex sections and the inevitable progressive rock syntax of quiet/loud dynamic, their unique ability to create mini-compositions of depth and almost bury them in a context like this speaks volumes. Thematically, the people's opinions have turned against the leader, whose compromises and lies are now obvious.

'The Face' (Shulman, Shulman, Minnear)
Featuring some busy interplay between violin, guitar and bass, and one of Derek's less attractive vocals, 'The Face' is another side of the politician's deceit; caught out and apologising but really only showing one of his many faces. While Derek's voice was strong, and he was an able singer, his strident approach can be mono-dimensional and is one of the notable flaws in the Gentle Giant sound, especially in the studio. In any case, 'The Sound' is a good chance for the group to kick out the jams a little with a brief guitar jam, behind which John is really cooking on drums and Ray is contributing his own distinctive bass riff.

'Valedictory' (Shulman, Shulman, Minnear)
In a capitulation of 'Proclamation', the leader goes back on his word: 'Things must stay, there must be no change.' It's a too-brief ending at only 3:21 and, as good as it is, it would have been great to end with

Right: *Part Of My Past* is a definitive introduction to the pre-Gentle Giant world of the Shulman brothers. *(EMI)*

Tree friends (ha-ha): The *Three Friends* line up with (left to right) Malcolm, Gary, Phil, Ray, Derek and Kerry.

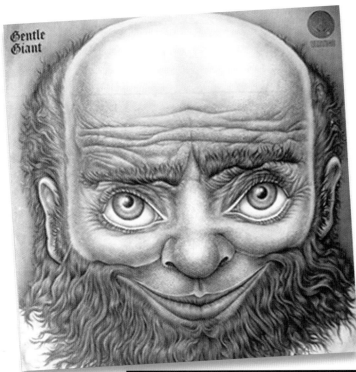

Left: George Underwood's distinctive artwork for the self-titled Gentle Giant debut on Vertigo with the actual 'giant'. *(Vertigo)*

Right: The controversial and widely derided 'arse-licking' cover of Gentle Giant's second album, *Acquiring The Taste*. *(Vertigo)*

Right: Confusingly, in the US and Canada, the cover of *Three Friends* was almost identical to their debut. *(Columbia)*

Left: The 'gentle giant' holding the assembled cast in his hands on the bottom of the US/Canadian cover of *Three Friends*. *(Columbia)*

Left: The sole Roger Dean Gentle Giant album cover artwork for *Octopus* doesn't resemble his work for the likes of Yes or Uriah Heep. *(Vertigo)*

Right: Bizarrely, the group's American record label commissioned a different cover (by graphic artist Charles White) for *Octopus* in the US. *(Columbia)*

Right: The distinctive cover for *In A Glass House* featured a plastic 'window' with 'negative' images of the boys in the band. *(Vertigo)*

Left: The original cover for *The Power And The Glory* with die-cut playing cards and curved top edges. *(Vertigo)*

Left: A publicity picture featuring the *Three Friends* era of the group. From left: Gary, Derek, Kerry, Ray, Malcolm and Phil.

Right: Gary, Ray and Derek (wearing that infamous white boiler suit) captured circa 1978.

Left: The slimmed-down lineup featuring Gary, John, Ray, Kerry and Derek and an arsenal of gear.

Gary doing his guitar thing live, July 1976 at Elyria, Ohio. *(David Knight)*

Above: Ray looking crazed in Cleveland, October 1974, where Gentle Giant opened for Golden Earring. *(David Knight)*

Below: Derek (right) in full frontal polyglottal mode captured in Akron, March 1975. *(David Knight)*

Above: Kerry in the middle of an intense vibraphonic workout, July 1976 at Elyria, Ohio. *(David Knight)*

Below: Ray looking intense as he takes a bass pause to add his voice to the mix, July 1976 at Elyria, Ohio. *(David Knight)*

Left: The 1975 album *Freehand* was their first release through Chrysalis and marked a shift to less complex structures. *(Chrysalis)*

Right: The group's 1976 album, *Interview*, tanked at the box office but they were on fine live form at this time. *(Chrysalis)*

Right: The double album *Playing The Fool*, recorded during the *Interview* tour and released in 1977, caught the group at its best. *(Chrysalis)*

Left: *The Missing Piece* (1977) felt like a misstep with it's a range of musical stabs in the dark but no clear direction. *(Chrysalis)*

Left: The power and the glory of Gentle Giant captured at their last British performance for BBC's *Sight & Sound* series. (*BBC*)

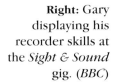

Right: Gary displaying his recorder skills at the *Sight & Sound* gig. (*BBC*)

Left: Gary, Ray, Derek (on bass) and Kerry doing their multiple 'geetarthing' at the *Sight & Sound* gig. (*BBC*)

Right: Derek's powerful voice was at its best in live performance, but here he's miming for the *Interview* promo.

Left: Gary, Ray, Derek (on baritone sax) and John seemingly hitting their stride in the *Interview* video promo.

Right: Ray plucking out a catgut melody on his trusty violin for the *Interview* promo.

Left: *Giant For A Day* (1978), with its novelty cover, is universally considered the group's worst album. *(Chrysalis)*

Right: *Civilian* (1980) found the group with a slick American-focused sound, but it was too little, too late. *(Chrysalis)*

Right: *Three Piece Suite* is a 2017 collection on Blu-ray/CD that gathers together Steven Wilson-remixed tracks from Gentle Giant's first three albums. *(Alucard)*

Left: *Unburied Treasure* is a mammoth limited edition box released late 2019, that offered all the studio work, loads of live performances as well as a book and ephemera. *(Alucard)*

Above: An American record company shot from the group's later years: Derek, Gary, Kerry, John, Ray.

Below: Three Friends, Gary's occasional Gentle Giant tribute band, with Malcolm Mortimore (drums) and Roger Carey (bass).

an epic musical recapitulation. Still, it bookends a classic album nicely and reinforces the theme, and the depressing idea that no matter what the era, the powerful individuals that we call leaders never live up to expectations.

Free Hand (1975)

Personnel:
Derek Shulman: lead and backing vocals, recorder, saxophone
Ray Shulman: bass, violin, viola, vocals
Kerry Minnear: Hammond organ, Minimoog, synthesizer, piano, electric
piano, clavinet, vibraphone, marimba, harpsichord, harp, cello, celesta,
glockenspiel, percussion, recorder, lead and backing vocals
Gary Green: acoustic guitar, electric guitar, recorder, vocals
John Weathers: drums, percussion
Produced at Advision, April 1975 by Gentle Giant, engineered by
Gary Martin
Release date: July 1975
Running time: 36.50

It was the beginning of fallow times for progressive rock, 1975 a fag-end
of a year that saw no releases from Yes or Emerson Lake and Palmer,
King Crimson's dissolution and the first stirrings of a back-to-basics
garage-rock movement that later got tagged 'punk'. It felt like there was
nowhere further to go for progressive rock: ironic, given the seemingly
endless creative potential of its beginnings.

This isn't the time or place to get into the specifics of the issues
around the genre's swift fall from favour, but suffice to say that
while many of their contemporaries had – through a combination of
circumstances – found themselves in a bad place, the hard-touring,
disciplined and determined Gentle Giant simply continued as though
nothing was amiss. This can probably be partly ascribed to the band's
unusual and near hermetic existence, but also because they were
neither operating on the top, high-stakes level of popularity, nor on the
struggling bottom. And because they were reliable and always gave a
good show, it was business as usual... for a while, at least.

The force was still with them on *Free Hand*, then. Their first post-
Vertigo album, recorded for new label Chrysalis, was a further
consolidation of the strengths forged on *The Power And The Glory*.
And while it wasn't quite as stellar as its predecessor, it displayed a
new, more hard-rocking aspect of the group. Most of Gentle Giant's
key characteristics were still intact, but the harder, more electric
sound inevitably saw the sweeter, more idiosyncratic aspects of Gentle
Giant sacrificed. In reality, this seventh Gentle Giant album showed a
remarkable run of rampant creativity and included a couple of cuts that
would become centrepieces of their live show.

While with each successive album, the group's production had become more sophisticated, it's worth noting the almost 10cc-like layering of *The Power And The Glory*, and *Free Hand* even more so. The fact that there's a quadraphonic mix of this album speaks volumes: while Gentle Giant had become so adept that they could record entire takes in the studio, they were also enticed by the studio-trickery of the times to partake of the sugar-coating that technology allowed. It's interesting that 10cc's *Original Soundtrack* came out the same year – a record the critics placed scorn on because of its emphasis on production values. That album contained the studio-perfect 'I'm Not In Love', and Queen's similarly studio shined 'Bohemian Rhapsody' hit the shops the same year. It was this environment into which *Free Hand* was hurled, although, like previous albums, it hardly made a mark in the group's homeland. It would be Gentle Giant's last great album, and the first and only of the group's albums to crack the *Billboard* top 50.

And remarkably, it also did respectable business in the UK. But bizarrely, instead of capitalising on its success in England, there was only one gig there, and instead, they ended up on an endless US tour that was hopelessly botched by the promoters. The band were billed with inappropriate co-headliners, often playing support to lumpen boogie bands, so when they should have been celebrating their high watermark they were sometimes booed offstage.

'Just The Same' (Shulman, Shulman, Minnear)

The album gets going with some finger-snapping and a familiar circular piano figure in an odd metre, together with a few bars of strummed guitar before the full band enters, along with Derek's vocal. As usual, there's a lot going on, including Ray's delicious bass modulations, the multi-tracked 'horn section', and Kerry's wiggly synthesizer.

The adjoining musical motif is as melodically distinctive as anything the band ever wrote, and then there's the mid-section, which sounds like the perfect theme with which to evoke a relaxing day at the beach, with its easy-listening guitar lines, synth strings and gently pulsing vibes. This then gets its groove-on, which is the cue for one of Kerry's rare synth solos, before returning to the original handclaps and Derek's unforgiving vocal.

The song itself seems to be aimed at anyone who would either look up to or idolise a band member. He's just doing what he wants to do. He's just like anyone else, except that he's in a band.

'On Reflection' (Shulman, Shulman, Minnear)

One of Gentle Giant's defining moments and a live highlight, 'On Reflection' is a veritable masterclass in counterpoint vocalese, with its declamatory 'All around!/all around!' line one of their most memorable moments. Not a second of its almost too-short 5:43 running time (described by the band as 'four pieces of a group-scribed fugue') is wasted, as the group expertly weaves its way through a set of changes that somehow, miraculously, hold together. The first part is sung by Derek, acappella (with distinct stereo separation), with the help of the group's harmonising (and very likely, overdubbing), then takes on another dimension as Kerry's more gentle serenading voice tells the sad tale of a romance that's dead in the water.

As with 'Just The Same', this is clearly a piece hewn out of the experience of being in a band, and the difficulty in sustaining long-term, serious relationships when living a markedly different way of life. Songs about being in a band can be boring and self-indulgent (as hilariously satirised by Frank Zappa in 'Road Ladies') but Gentle Giant approach the subject with sensitivity, and there's none of the usual complaining about the rigours of their chosen profession. It's a gorgeous piece with a clear message for anyone wanting to get involved with a touring musician: accept them, don't try to change them, and know what you're getting into.

Just when you're thinking there will be no rocking out, towards the end there's a very tasty guitar/organ duet that leads into a victorious resolution; indicative, perhaps, that the relationship split was, indeed, for the best.

'Free Hand' (Shulman, Shulman, Minnear)

The intro to 'Free Hand' is a ruse, starting as it does with a pleasant, jazzy guitar and keyboard interplay. In fact, (most of) the title track is a boiling, restless rocker with those relentless Gentle Giant melodic repetitions and the kind of emphasised riffing that typified parts of *In A Glass House*. There's more wriggle-room than usual for Gary's exquisitely disciplined guitar work, and some typically inventive, complex keyboard machinations from Kerry.

Led by Derek's angry-sounding vocals, it's thematically a variation on 'On Reflection', except that piece was a gentle examination of what went wrong, whereas this is full of accusation and ire and musical muscle. He's over with her games and lies and has a clear head and a free hand to move on.

'Time To Kill' (Shulman, Shulman, Minnear)

'Time To Kill' finds our protagonist free of the bonds that held him, alone but not wasting time. While featuring a little counterpoint singing, the musical tenor of the piece is quite different from typical Gentle Giant. For instance, the descending notes of a 'choir' behind Derek on the verses and indeed some of the guitar moves are more redolent, once again, of 10cc than anything. They display a slickness in tune with that year, and the studios that produced the big hits to which we have already referred.

It's an interesting diversion from the typical Gentle Giant tropes with the usual attention to detail and adds depth to the album experience without ever quite attaining greatness. And unfortunately, the slight disco-soul feel to the piece sounds out of place.

'His Last Voyage' (Shulman, Shulman, Minnear)

The album's longest track at 6:26, this piece begins with gentle guitar/bass/vibes extrapolations and Kerry's angelic vocals, which bloom into counterpoint. The first three minutes coasts along on this jazz-oriented bed, until the drums kick in and give the voyage some heft. It's an odd concoction, but it works beautifully. Kerry's layered vocals hover over the groove until finally, Gary's guitar lashes out with a gnarly solo, and the piano becomes more jagged, in a modernist jazz style reminiscent of Keith Tippett's work on King Crimson's *Lizard*.

Lyrically, this piece is as bleak as it gets, but it's typically clear-headed: try as you might, it seems to be saying, whatever you do or whoever you end up with, death will get you in the end. But maybe it's not so bleak. 'On Reflection' noted that the experience was the thing, not the destination.

One of the low-key highlights of a really great and often overlooked album, 'His Last Voyage' shows that while the group has made some concessions to popular taste on *Free Hand*, they're yet to compromise their essential character.

'Talybont' (Shulman, Shulman, Minnear)

One of the most endearing tracks in the Gentle Giant catalogue and a rare instrumental outing, 'Talybont' is an all-too-brief (2:40) opportunity for Kerry to mimic a medieval shindig on his synth rig. It's hard to figure out what's real and what's electronic, but this folksy ditty features what sounds like echoed Moog, bass, guitar and recorders.

The band could probably have made a career out of modernising medieval folk minstrelsy but chose a fusion that was wholly original, to their credit. If this track had shown the way to a more successful path for Gentle Giant – television theme tunes, perhaps? – it would have diluted their firepower. As it is, it stands as a very cute diversion.

'Mobile' (Shulman, Shulman, Minnear)

Having spent the majority of the album's theme exploring the dissolution of relationships caused by their chosen lifestyle, 'Mobile' is simply a statement of fact, a description of life on the road. While it adds little that we didn't already know, at least they don't dwell on feeling sorry for themselves. Going back and forth between an acoustic jig on violin and guitar and a heavy, somewhat mundane rock groove, it's not Gentle Giant's greatest moment or a particularly exciting way to finish the album, but perhaps they needed this particular backdrop to reflect the lyrical subject matter musically.

As it is, the piece is still packed with the requisite detail, and for those looking past the bare bones of the track, there's some particularly adept fiddling by Ray and the group's always surprising propensity for unusual nodules of interesting musicality in the places you'd least expect them.

In'terview (1976)

Personnel:
Derek Shulman: lead and backing vocals, recorder, saxophone, percussion
Ray Shulman: bass, violin, guitar, percussion, vocals
Kerry Minnear: Hammond organ, Minimoog, synthesizer, piano, electric
piano, Clavinet, marimba, percussion, lead and backing vocals
Gary Green: acoustic guitar, electric guitar, recorder, vocals
John Weathers: drums, backing vocals
Produced at Advision, Feb to March 1976 by Gentle Giant, engineered by
Gary Martin
Release date: April 23, 1976
Running time: 36.47

What do you do when the music press mostly ignores you? If you're
Gentle Giant, you create a concept album around the laborious process
of conducting promotional interviews. If they wanted to ensure that
they would get offside with the critical fraternity, they couldn't have
opted for a better conceptual conceit. And so begins the slow slide
to oblivion. It's hard to fathom just how the *In'terview* concept came
about, or who green-lighted it. Maybe the group were just so jaded by
the road and so angry at their lack of recognition in the UK, that this
seeming deathwish seemed somehow like a good idea.

In a sense, it's comparable to *Three Friends*: an album with a fairly
weak concept that fails to inspire the best songs. And while *Free
Hand* had its share of songs about being in a band and specifically
the difficulties in maintaining romantic relationships when you are,
In'terview fails the litmus test by getting dragged down in boring
complaint. Inevitably, the album coincided with a downturn in their
fortunes, and it wasn't well received. And that's a great pity because
it isn't at all bad. While it's not a patch on *The Power And The Glory*
or *Free Hand*, there's still a world of invention within the songs, as
long as you ignore the heavy-handed lyrical content. The *In'terview*
tour that followed certainly showed that the group still had it in them,
and it was that tour that resulted in one of the best live albums ever
released by any band, *Playing The Fool*.

'Interview' (Shulman, Shulman, Minnear)

The album and its title track begin with a preamble to a radio interview,
followed by one of the group's more overtly muscular grooves. Its
instrumental sections are noticeably less complex than previous albums,

71

though they're still packed with quirk and invention. For instance, after the somewhat predictable (by now) path followed by Derek's vocals, there's some intentionally wonky syncopation between John's percussion and Kerry's barrelhouse piano, followed by a quiet interlude of guitar and organ interplay, a rare appearance by John on some vocal lines, and then... well, it shoots off into what can only be called a funk groove with an avant-garde piano solo! As if that's not enough for one song, there's mutant rubber band bass and fake sitar with whispers going on in the background, which are then joined by some halting organ. Eventually, the song returns to its main theme and Derek's vocal line, over which Kerry drapes some extra fruity organ and string synth.

While the subject – a band wondering why they get asked the same dull questions over and over again – isn't endearing, the song itself is prime Gentle Giant, proving that they've got plenty of life left in them.

'Give It Back' (Shulman, Shulman, Minnear)

Unfortunately, 'Give It Back' is out of character and its attempt at a reggae lope a serious miscalculation. Reggae was booming at the time, and it's easy to see the appeal, and why everyone from Eric Clapton ('I Shot The Sheriff') to 10cc ('Dreadlock Holiday') tried their hand at the style. And it's not that Gentle Giant doesn't do it well: clearly, this was one of the most adept and musically versatile music units ever assembled. No, it's simply that stylistically, it stands out like a sore thumb and doesn't gel with the musical character that's been well established over six years. That, and the fact that reggae is built on a certain looseness rhythmically that – while easily replicated by Ray and John – doesn't fit so easily with Derek's stiffly enunciated lyrics.

But still, it's an interesting failure. While lyrically it appears to bemoan the financial ups and downs of band life and the incorrect perceptions of the music press, the simpler style provides a few opportunities for Kerry to plant some especially tasty synthesizer melodies and well-placed sound effects.

It is, however, sobering to reflect on the musical straitjacket that they'd built for themselves. While the musical influences that fed into Gentle Giant's sound included blues, hard rock, jazz fusion, classical (mostly baroque and medieval) and several other genres, the way they applied these influences gave them a very specific sound that couldn't easily be backed away from. In the case of Genesis, for instance, the more opaque 'classical' form of their music was easily commercialised when the time came. Perhaps Gentle Giant had become stuck because they were simply too distinctive, and too defined by their medieval aspects.

'Design' (Shulman, Shulman, Minnear)

Speaking of which, 'Design' is a return to the layered counterpoint and the associated medieval feel, and in contrast to 'Give It Back', it's a prime piece of Gentle Giant.

Starting with another 'interview' segment ('How would you describe your music?' asks the interviewer, to which the response is a muddled mess of murmuring), it features a lovely Kerry vocal with ethereal harmonies wafting over the sound field, and the effect is magical. Then comes a highly percussive section featuring Derek as the lead voice on an unusual piece of vocal harmonising. Despite the use of the by-now-expected counterpoint, the way it's constructed is fresh and invigorating, especially at its explosive end.

Lyrically, the narrator is rueing his life having passed without having achieved the gratification he was sure would come his way. The sobering subject matter hardly puts a dent on this special piece.

'Another Show' (Shulman, Shulman, Minnear)

The momentum and excitement is maintained on 'Another Show', which starts out like a runaway train with its demonically pitch-bent organ, fast tempo and a frantic vocal by Derek. The music obviously attempts to capture the head-spinning feeling of a band travelling rough and playing a never-ending series of dates. The sense of an ongoing state of flux and psychic distress is palpable on a piece that doesn't really develop as much as simply continue on its runaway course.

'Empty City' (Shulman, Shulman, Minnear)

It's not exactly clear how this song ties in with the interview concept. 'Empty City' is about a woman who 'knows the streets where she walks, never were paved with gold' who packs up and leaves the empty city. Is she a prostitute, a groupie? Who knows? In any case, it's one of the album's more reflective songs, with some beautiful acoustic fingerpicking from Gary and a deftly played shift of moods and modes, from the melodic, harmony-enriched first verse to the more strident second verse with blaring double-tracked saxophones, and the following rather fluid – if too brief – electric guitar solo.

Although there are the usual Gentle Giant musical phrases, there's a real sense here of the group's potential for developing a less musically complex but moodier, textural approach to song construction.

'Timing' (Shulman, Shulman, Minnear)

Back to the 'interview', it's the classic 'how would you describe the music you play?' question, and into a lyric that seems to be questioning the process; the need for the timing to be just right in this cat and mouse game between the press and the artist.

Musically, this is almost a power-pop song, albeit one that's packed with more elements than one that would ever stand a hope of charting. But it's certainly more accessible and geared towards the 'rawk' crowd that they were courting on their never-ending American tours.

'I Lost My Head' (Shulman, Shulman, Minnear)

Although again not lyrically explicit, 'I Lost My Head' appears to be chronicling a sexual union where he gave more of himself than he was accustomed to. Or did he lose his head in an interview, and give the person more than he'd planned to? It's not clear.

It's an odd way to finish the record. While it ends on a relatively buoyant note, the piece doesn't really go anywhere or do anything of consequence. It all starts well enough with some nice interplay between acoustic guitar and harpsichord and a falsetto vocal from Kerry, and the melodic theme (restated with harpsichord and recorder) is elegant and memorable.

At the three-minute mark of this seven-minute piece, the group starts pounding away on one of its less memorable riffs, which closely resembles a sea shanty, and Derek's vocal is less than inspiring. Even here, however, there are a few instrumental twists and turns that make this lesser piece (and therefore an inauspicious ending) worth hearing.

Playing The Fool – The Official Live

Personnel:
Derek Shulman: lead vocals, saxophone, recorder, bass, percussion
Ray Shulman: bass, vocals, violin, guitar, trumpet, recorder, percussion
Kerry Minnear: Electric piano, Clavinet, Moog synthesizer, Hammond
organ, cello, vibraphone, recorder, percussion, vocals
Gary Green: acoustic guitar, electric guitar, vocals, recorder, percussion
John Weathers: drums, percussion, vocals, vibraphone, tambourine
Recorded September 23 to October 7, 1976, in Dusseldorf, Paris, Brussels
and Munich
Release date: January 18, 1977
Running time: 78:09

It's instructive to see the video evidence of the live Gentle Giant
captured on the two available DVDs (*Giant On The Box* and *GG At
The GG*), and *Playing The Fool* captures the animated and aggressive
concert manifestation of the group without the impediment of cameras.

The only live album released during the group's lifetime, this double
vinyl might have been enough to kick-start a revival of their fortunes
had it been released a few years before, but its January 1977 release
date meant that it was unleashed on a scene suddenly awash with punk
rock. Nevertheless, internationally it was one of Gentle Giant's more
popular releases (it climbed to number 89 on the *Billboard* charts), and
for good reason. *Playing The Fool* was recorded during the *In'terview*
tour but wisely eschews that album in favour of an unerringly strong
selection of material from earlier releases.

While the Gentle Giant studio albums are deftly layered and often
feature overdubs, this is an opportunity to hear their songs rearranged
for live performance. Apparently, the album does contain a few
clavinet overdubs simply because the original was subject to electrical
interference, but is otherwise warts-and-all, and is all the better for
it. There's not a moment of flab in these performances recorded in
Munich, Brussels, Paris and Dusseldorf between September 23 and
October 7, 1976. The group is tight, muscular and in peak form, and the
audience is audibly appreciative without being intrusive.

Some have claimed that this is one of the best live albums ever
recorded, and I back that assertion. The performances are superb,
vocally the group are in top form, and the sound quality is good
enough to convey both the musicality and the spontaneous excitement.
Highlights? Well, there's not a better 'Excerpts From Octopus' out

there, and at 15 minutes and 39 seconds, there's probably nothing better to win over a brand new fan. Where many live albums contain near-identical versions of studio favourites with the annoying addition of audience noise, *Playing The Fool* gives us a generous sampling of radically reimagined versions of old favourites. This is the case with the 10:20 rendition of 'So Sincere', which features a dynamic drum freakout.

Unlike most of their progressive rock contemporaries, when Gentle Giant performed live they weren't just revving up their album arrangements with a bit of adrenaline, but often omitting parts or adding whole new sections or performing a particular line on a different instrument. Unique moments? On the second disc, the group briefly play the old song 'Sweet Georgia Brown' (titled 'Breakdown In Brussels') during an equipment breakdown. Veritably a 'greatest hits' (or non-hits) done live with extra verve, *Playing The Fool* remains one of the group's most essential albums.

'Just The Same' (Shulman, Shulman, Minnear)
This opener fades in to audience noise and what sounds like a taped intro. Immediately it's apparent that the layering is sacrificed, but in its place is boundless energy and excitement. Kerry's electric piano figures, Ray's rollicking bass and John's pounding drums provide an immediate rush, while Gary's gorgeous melodic guitar lines add an emotional aspect before Kerry contributes a squiggly solo. Derek's vocal is so perfect that he makes the unnatural need for perfect timing and intonation seem easy.

'Proclamation/Valedictory' (Shulman, Shulman, Minnear)
'Just The Same' segues seamlessly into 'Proclamation/Valedictory'. Kerry's Clavinet is more evident than on the studio recording, and the mind-bending vocal harmonies aren't as rich, but they're still spectacular. The quiet mid-section is dumped, and as the song reaches its midpoint, there's a palpable 'live' feeling that gives it a sense of drama quite different from the studio recording with its substantially modified instrumentation.

'On Reflection' (Shulman, Shulman, Minnear)
There's a fade-out before 'On Reflection', which is radically redrawn for live performance. Starting out with delicate recorders, violin, cello and chimes, the instrumental section is drawn-out before the famous Derek-led a cappella vocal. As Kerry's lovely voice was considered 'weak' in a

concert context (he was more of a close-miked crooner) Derek takes the lead. Once again, while the studio version has a precision that this version lacks, it's worth hearing (and comparing) both.

'Excerpts From Octopus' (Shulman, Shulman, Shulman, Minnear)
One of the most impressive sections of *Playing The Fool* is this six-song medley-type selection from *Octopus*. Another fade-out (and in) and we get the famous rolling coin sound effect before a rollicking (but short) version of 'The Boys In The Band'. Completely revised instrumentally from the studio versions, there's an extended acoustic guitar duo between Gary and Ray, featuring 'Raconteur Troubadour.' Before it lulls us too much, it's a quick run-through of 'Acquiring The Taste' and into 'Knots', which is every bit as phenomenal as the studio version with its multi-part vocal harmonies and contrapuntal instrumental parts. I would have assumed this was impossible to perform adequately live, and it must have been spine-tingling to witness it in the flesh. Kerry's Dr Phibes organ/synth lines deliver a bridge between 'Knots' and 'Ocean Bridge' and 'The Advent Of Panurge' which rocks and grooves hard while eventually making way for the famous 'recorder quartet'. There's probably no better introduction to the world of Gentle Giant than this fifteen minutes and 35 seconds of superb distinctiveness.

'Funny Ways' (Minnear, Shulman, Shulman, Shulman)
You know it's live when you can hear an 'earth' buzz as the track starts. Taking on Kerry's softer vocal lines as well as his more strident ones, Derek displays both his ability to cut through the music but also his ability to apply some subtlety where required. No doubt, his soul and R&B background came into huge use here. On this song from their first album, Ray gets out his trumpet and Kerry gets into an extended vibraphone solo. Were they tired of playing this 1970 song by 1976? Who knows, but it sounds fresh and dynamic and still as experimental and mysterious as it did when it was first recorded, but with extra firepower, especially from John's drumming.

'The Runaway' (Shulman, Shulman, Minnear)
'This album was called *In A Glass House*', announces Derek at the beginning of Disc 2, as the taped breaking glass sound effects begin. The Clavinet here (unlike the album) isn't harshly recorded, and the organ is more clearly audible. In fact, the song benefits in some ways

from a less detailed mix, as it's a piece with a rollicking rock undertow
and a lot of kick.

'Experience' (Shulman, Shulman, Minnear)

'The Runaway' segues into 'Experience', which once again, loses little
from its studio counterpart and gains some live excitement. Because
so much of *In A Glass House* sounded like it was thrashed out live,
these songs translate well to a concert setting with their rock energy
and John's pronounced swing. Once again, in the quiet passages you
can hear the dirty buzz of 1970s gear through a 1970s PA that would
have been – somewhat to its detriment – digitally extracted from a 21st
Century recording.

'So Sincere' (Shulman, Shulman, Minnear)

An epic 10:20 version of this classic from *The Power And The Glory*
that, once again, substitutes some instruments and tones to render
it effective in a live context. It's a rare chance for Gary to cut loose
with some florid guitar extemporisation over Kerry's choppy Clavinet.
There's even a sizzling, octopus-like drum solo that evolves into an
'everyone on deck' percussion jamboree, with some pretty xylophone
working up to a full and powerful bout of thumping. There's some
audience whooping towards the end that was apparently provoked by
Kerry wiggling his derriere in the direction of the crowd.

'Free Hand'

Given that *Free Hand* was still fairly recent when this was recorded,
this is a fairly faithful live version of its title track. It's nice to hear Gary
once again cut loose with a cool wah-wah guitar solo, although it's fairly
brief. That the kind of riff structures the group had established with *In
A Glass House,* are further developed on *Free Hand* is very evident on
hearing it live.

'Sweet Georgia Brown (Breakdown In Brussels)'

Drummed up on the hoof when there was a power failure to Kerry's
keyboards, this spontaneous respite from original Gentle Giant material
is performed acoustically, with Ray carrying the melody with his violin.
It shows just how nimble and quick on their feet and versatile they
were, in that they were able to instantly fashion a rather playful version
of this 1925 jazz standard. But as with their oft-performed 'Octopus
highlights' flute rendition of 'Yankee Doodle Dandy', there's something

else that simply has to be said about this. It may seem a bit corny to generations raised in later decades on groups like Radiohead where any levity or sense of humour is wholly omitted, but it's a demonstration of the group's desire to *entertain*. Progressive rock bands were roundly criticized for their supposed pretentiousness by the music press when descriptions like 'musically ambitious' and 'adventurous' are much more accurate. In a sense, while progressive rock was indeed at times edgy and experimental, it was seldom up its own arse, and in Gentle Giant's case, there was a very real sense of fun.

'Peel The Paint/I Lost My Head'
This combination of one of the highlights of *Three Friends* with one of the highlights of *In'terview* (the only song included from the group's then-latest album) sounds a bit muddy and tacked on, but is still great. Was it an encore piece, I wonder?

The Missing Piece (1977)
Personnel:
Derek Shulman: lead vocals
Ray Shulman: bass, guitar, percussion
Kerry Minnear: Hammond organ, Minimoog, synthesizer, piano, electric
piano, clavinet, percussion, vocals
Gary Green: acoustic guitar, electric guitar
John Weathers: drums
Produced at Relight, May 1977 by Gentle Giant, engineered by Gary Martin
Release date: August 26, 1977
Running time: 36.28

In'terview, it turned out, would be the last necessary Gentle Giant album.
Three more would follow before the band called it quits, but *The Missing
Piece*, *Giant For A Day* and *Civilian* are all examples of a group that had
lost its *raison d'être*, and they were accordingly stylistically confused.
What were they thinking? It appears that in the light of the increasing
commercialisation of rock in America and the sudden sprouting of punk
in England that they were inspired to try on some new musical clothing.
Unfortunately for them, the clothes just didn't fit. While not as tragi-comic
as Emerson, Lake and Palmer's disastrous, out of character *Love Beach*,
The Missing Piece feels compromised and muddled.

Ironically, however, on its own terms, this non-performing release
is pretty good. Any normal rock band would have been proud to have
achieved an album containing such an adept and eclectic selection of
tunes, all of them (of course) performed expertly and enthusiastically.
Perhaps if Gentle Giant hadn't been typecast as 'that medieval prog
band' they'd have had a hit on their hands, and several of the songs
were certainly strong enough to have been hit singles. Maybe if they'd
changed their name and assumed pseudonyms, the music media might
have listened to the album without preconceptions, but the Shulman
brothers had already been down that road with Simon Dupree And The
Big Sound when they released a single as The Moles.

But realistically, success was never going to come their way. Many of
Gentle Giant's progressive rock contemporaries had already collapsed
by this point – not killed by punk as is widely rumoured, but for a
variety of reasons that we don't have the time to go into here. The
most successful were those few who had made a smooth transition
to a more pop-oriented sound, the obvious example being Genesis.
This also applies to their former singer, Peter Gabriel, who was able

to launch his solo career as a kind of new wave hybrid. Having a clear direction and real consistency allowed Genesis and Gabriel both to keep huge portions of their previous fanbase and make legions of new ones who barely knew the word 'prog'.Gentle Giant, as a second division progressive rock group that had never broken through to mass acceptance or recognition, were simply not in a position to transition successfully. Consequently, *The Missing Piece* is like nine stabs in the dark by several different groups with different stylistic tendencies. Each song has its merits, but...

And, of course, it tanked. For the first time, it felt like the wheels were coming off.

'Two Weeks In Spain' (Shulman, Shulman, Minnear)

What a shock for long-time fans: 'Two Weeks In Spain' is far removed from the sound Gentle Giant had propagated in their first six years and eight albums. Featuring a simple, nagging chorus that today would be called an ear-worm, it's a spritely jaunt that feels unnaturally sun-flecked and too-happy for a band that had cultivated a dark edge and a sound with plenty of minor chords.

With its bland lyric about a holiday in Spain and Thin Lizzy-style, creamy dual-attack guitar from Gary, it all comes across as a little forced. Listen past the main elements of this blatant attempt to find new fans and there are still remnants of the Gentle Giant we know and love. It certainly gives Gary the opportunity to demonstrate his remarkable versatility and in the brief time available on a song that only lasts in its entirely a mere 3:07, Kerry produces some impressively symphonic keyboard colourings.

'I'm Turning Around' (Shulman, Shulman, Minnear)

Speaking of Genesis/Gabriel, on 'I'm Turning Around' it's as if Kerry and the Shulman brothers had set out to replicate that sound. This memorable power ballad – a grown-up love song looking at a relationship with a fresh perspective/commitment – has an almost hymnal feeling. With Kerry's churchy electric piano and organ and a chorus full of symphonic pomp and splendour, it sounds like the hit that wasn't. It's not the Gentle Giant we know and love, but they do it well.

'Betcha Thought We Couldn't Do It' (Shulman, Shulman, Minnear)

And then, this. Oh dear. The self-referential lyrics make a pitch for accepting them on their own terms for what they're now doing.

We've been waiting such a long, long time.
To fit the pattern, fill the rhyme.
Now we can't stick in our old ways.

Fair enough, but this failed attempt at punking themselves up, sounds more like a hashed old rock'n'roll trope – lots of noise but the 'energy' sounds fake, as does Derek's attempt at a yobbish accent. Easily a contender for Gentle Giant's worst song, the only thing it really has going for it is a running time of only 2:23.

'Who Do You Think You Are?' (Shulman, Shulman, Minnear)
The dual guitar is back on this dreary rocker, which pokes fun at the insincerity of Hollywood hook-ups and guestlists. The Gentle Giant characteristics are repressed and backgrounded and while the rhythm section is enjoyably solid, and there are tantalising keyboard moments, this could really be one of the hundreds of wannabe rock bands from the mid-to-late 1970s.

'Mountain Time' (Shulman, Shulman, Minnear)
A song about being horny and hooking up, this sounds like an attempt to go all disco-funk, and it's just wrong. They're hugely competent at this propulsive stuff, and could probably have done it with their eyes shut, but who really needs to hear something that sounds like the Grease Band or Bonnie Bramlett on steroids? Oddly, it even includes female backing singers, who remain uncredited.

It's hard to imagine how the great Gentle Giant got to this odd juncture. Was it record company pressure to come up with a hit? Or did it represent a passing passion for one of the band members? We'll probably never know.

'As Old As You're Young (Shulman, Shulman, Minnear)
At last, something approximating the Gentle Giant sound, with its baroque Moog intro and Kerry's only vocal on the whole album. Their sound has been radically modified, however. Gone are the acoustic instruments together with any musical diversions, and the whole thing reeks of enforced happiness, a too-pat, jaunty flavour that matches the rather humdrum lyric, which is pretty much summed up by its title.

There's the merest hint of counterpoint and, although Kerry's keyboards are pleasant, and there's some nice interplay between the keys and Gary's arpeggiated guitar, it all somehow feels like diminishing returns. Eventually, Derek joins in for a verse or two, after which Kerry plays an outro of church-like organ.

'Memories Of Old Days' (Shulman, Shulman, Minnear)

By far the longest track at 7:18, this deeply reflective piece is again untypical, despite a slight aroma of medievalism in the (stereo) double-tracked guitar section. The real difference is that this time, it works. It's one of the group's rare mood pieces, where fancy playing is sacrificed to scene-setting and evocative, emotive sounds that relay a sense of peace, and it's completely devoid of drums.

It's a gorgeous thing with some fine acoustic guitar from Gary and the flute-sounding keyboards that have an almost Celtic flavour. With its surging organ, the sporadic appearance of the sounds of school children and an open-hearted vibe, 'Memories Of Old Days' is one of the few tracks that could have made the grade on a previous Gentle Giant album.

'Winning' (Shulman, Shulman, Minnear)

A subject that must have been close to the collective heart of Gentle Giant, 'Winning' looks at someone who has accumulated vast wealth but has ended up a Howard Hughes-like hideaway. So, what does 'winning' mean? Is the experience of trying the important thing? It's a great subject for a song, but musically, it seems confused about what it wants to be. Derek shouts out the words with conviction, but the musical clamour underneath lacks the usual clarity or power.

If only they'd figured out how to best utilise the arsenal of dynamic percussion that begins and ends the piece, perhaps keeping it spare and all the more powerful for it.You can't help wondering if the ultimate failure of 'Winning' and 'As Old As You're Young' have a lot to do with the group's shift from the familiar environment of Advision studio and relocation to an alien environment at Relight Studio in Holland.

'For Nobody' (Shulman, Shulman, Minnear)

At last, a full-on, thrusting take on the real Gentle Giant. It's just that here it's all vastly simplified and therefore, much less interesting. This is a shiny FM version of the group, where it's still okay for Ray's bass to play actual notes and for fancy keyboard arpeggios (as long as they're really short) but the momentum must be kept at all costs.

It's interesting to note that there's a short vocal section that once would have been an excuse for some stunning harmonising, but here it's truncated, phased and ends up sounding like the overdubbed power vocals of an American AOR group like Jefferson Starship, or something similar. It's all taken at a frantic pace, no doubt influenced by the energy of punk, while the slickness of the music itself is probably closer to American FM rock like Boston or Foreigner. How the mighty had fallen!

Giant For A Day (1978)

Personnel:
Derek Shulman: lead vocals
Ray Shulman: bass, guitar, backing vocals
Kerry Minnear: Hammond organ, Minimoog, synthesizer, piano, electric piano, xylophone, Clavinet, bass, vocals
Gary Green: acoustic guitar, electric guitar, backing vocals
John Weathers: drums, vocals
Produced at Ramport, Maison Rouge, Scorpio Sound, April-May 1978 by Gentle Giant
Release date: September 11, 1978
Running time: 35.33

If the hallmarks of the Gentle Giant sound were struggling to be heard on *The Missing Piece*, they're entirely missing in action on *Giant For A Day*. Oddly, after recording and releasing the album, the group failed to tour it and effectively took a long sabbatical between this resounding flop and what would turn out to be their final album, 1980's *Civilian*.

Any hardcore Gentle Giant fan is going to want to ask questions about how the band got to this place, and why they made this album – stripped as it was of all the elements long-term fans loved about the group – only to decide not to tour it. Oddly, there were some misguided attempts at merchandising and promotions using elements of its cover design. Perhaps it was this that the group figured could make up for its lack of live appearances. Almost certainly one of the most ignominious slow fades of any great band, the double blow of bad albums that's *Giant For A Day* and *Civilian* certainly gave them few new fans, despite the huge commercial concessions they'd made on them.

It must have been particularly sad for Kerry, as he's left with little to do of any real consequence, and must have felt rather like a loose wheel, after being the architect and hub of much of the greatest music the band created in its best years. The fact that it was recorded in no less than three studios is indicative of a band who no longer feel anchored in a safe place in which to explore their musical world. The result is an album that's probably best left on the shelf if you don't want your enthusiasm for the band dented.

'Words From The Wise' (Shulman, Shulman, Minnear)
The power-pop/rock on display here is streamlined and contains not a hint of what Gentle Giant once was. Instead, it's a shiny, gleaming AOR

rock sound that's closer to Boston or Chicago or some other corporate American product with a city for a name. It doesn't help that Derek's vocal is only one component of a fruity harmony style reminiscent of Crosby, Stills and Nash.

The best that can best said of it is that 'Words From The Wise' is highly competent, and had they not been saddled with their own history, perhaps they might just have been able to compete on what was then the mainstream American rock scene.

'Thank You' (Shulman, Shulman, Minnear)

Trying yet another hat on for size, on 'Thank You' they swap the gleaming AOR moves for some likeable down-home folk-rock with a strummed acoustic guitar and a slide guitar solo that makes them sound like try-outs for Neil Young's backing band. Musically, this is as basic as Gentle Giant ever got, and you can't help feeling sorry for Kerry, whose keyboards here, and elsewhere on this album, seem lost for anything palpable to contribute.

Lyrically, the band has shaved off all complexity as well, and this is a simple 'thank you' to a woman who has stuck with her man through thick and thin. However, it's interesting hearing Derek in a more rustic setting and not having to project his voice over a small orchestra for a change.

'Giant For A Day!' (Shulman, Shulman, Minnear)

With its lyrics about trying on different masks and assuming different identities as you like, it's not such a stretch of the imagination that the title track is literally about the band's new direction. Unfortunately, it's one of the least focused pieces on the album, managing to combine echoed rock and roll vocals with Thin Lizzy-style dual guitar and an almost punk-like guitar/keyboard riff. By the time the bombastic beat enters the picture, it's all sounding like it desperately needs a re-imagining.

'Spooky Boogie' (Shulman, Shulman, Minnear)

An uncharacteristic, brief (2:55) instrumental that piles on the Hammer horror. There's a beautifully slinky groove, punctuated by screams, and then midway, Kerry gets to do his thing on various keyboards and xylophone on a cartoonish-sounding theme. 'Spooky Boogie' is fun, if hardly Grade-A Gentle Giant fare, and it may have been a better way to finish the album.

'Take Me' (Derek Shulman, John Weathers)
John Weathers gets a co-writing, co-singing credit on 'Take Me', a request for a good woman to rescue the bloke from a life of bad living. With its unresolved, meandering verses and horribly American-sounding power-pop choruses, it cries out for some serious work-shopping. There's little else that can be said about a song that sounds as if the band lack the conviction to turn it into something worth hearing. On the other hand, the chorus could be described as an 'ear-worm'. But then again, repetition's like that.

'Little Brown Bag' (Shulman, Shulman, Minnear)
Sadly, it gets worse before it gets better. Listening to this song in 1978, long-time fans must have been shocked at hearing the kind of music that one always assumed the group were opposed to. 'Little Brown Bag' is a mundane boogie-rock piece with brash rock and roll guitar and Kerry doing his best to pound his keys like Jerry Lee Lewis, but ending up somewhat submerged under the ordinariness of it all.

'Friends' (John Weathers)
On which John Weathers gets his big chance: a solo vocal on his own song. The drummer acquits himself better than expected, his vocal coming over like an amateur Kerry, and his unpretentious song is impossible to dislike. It helps that the piece hinges on Gary's terrific acoustic guitar picking. This is simple folk music, and it does what it sets out to do admirably.

'No Stranger' (Shulman, Shulman, Minnear)
Derek's vocal melody, the electric piano, the backing harmonies, the overall structure all make this song sound like a tribute to 10cc. This gently loping song is again out of character, but like 'Friends', at least sits easily in their catalogue, unlike those pastiches of commercial American power pop.

'It's Only Goodbye' (Shulman, Shulman, Minnear)
Gary's guitar line sounds like it's trying for the kind of gravity Eric Clapton achieved with 'Layla' on this 'end of affair' power ballad. In fact, that Derek and The Dominoes classic is impossible to get out of your mind when listening to 'It's Only Goodbye', which is really only excusable as a tribute.

'Rock Climber' (Shulman, Shulman, Minnear)

Once again, this ode to a mysterious groupie/one-night-stand could – if one were being kind – be compared to the kind of sly insinuating satire that 10cc traded in earlier in the '70s, but it lacks that group's pop smarts and integration. Instead, it's as if the verse and chorus are welded together from different songs, Derek wielding his least attractive shouty voice, and it all feels like a bum note on which to end.

Civilian (1980)

Personnel:
Derek Shulman: lead vocals
Ray Shulman: bass, acoustic guitar, backing vocals
Kerry Minnear: Hammond organ, synthesizer, electric piano, Clavinet, vocals
Gary Green: electric guitar
John Weathers: drums, backing vocals
Produced at Sound City, Van Nuys, California, August to November 1979 by Gentle Giant, Engineer – Geoff Emerick
Release date: March 3, 1980
Running time: 32:41

What a way to go. After the longest ever pause between albums, Gentle Giant released what would turn out to be their final studio album in March 1980. Critical and consumer reaction to *Civilian* was reportedly so negative that some stores refused to stock it at all. After the lay-off, they made the ill-advised decision to reconvene, and the result would be a record that bore scant relation to the Gentle Giant sound that its fans knew and loved. If *The Missing Piece* and *Giant For A Day* saw the group thrashing about in shallow waters, seeking a way forward and trying on different styles for size, *Civilian* was, however, at least partially successful on its own terms.

The album was recorded at the famed Sound City Studios in California – a legendary studio documented by Dave Grohl in the 2013 documentary, *Sound City* – with former Beatles engineer Geoff Emerick on board. It's fair to assume that the group was at least optimistic that a swish American studio and the engineer who did so much to make *Abbey Road* one of the best-sounding albums ever released would provide a fertile stomping ground. Sadly, however, by this point the group had expunged much of its tonal and timbral variety by ditching its acoustic instruments and reducing their musical palette down to that of a bog-standard rock band. The record was never going to sound great because by this point their music was streamlined, slick, American-style radio rock with a slightly hard-rock edge.

Kerry, especially, must have been gnashing his teeth through boredom, as the perfunctory rock demanded of this edition of the group barely needed his performative or creative interjections at all. Even the passage of time hasn't improved *Civilian*, which is considerably more cogent than the previous two albums but also offers less of interest overall.

'Convenience (Clean And Easy)' (Shulman, Shulman, Minnear)
It's ironic that on 'Convenience', Derek's critiquing plastic consumer
society and how it runs like one big machine, but doing so with a sound
that's homogenised to fit that machine. On one level, it's a shot of
energy and appears to show renewed focus. It's probable that – with the
monotonous beat and electronic bleeping – they had come under the
influence of heavily ironic post-punk groups like Devo. But if the new
wave aesthetic had permeated Gentle Giant's musical infrastructure, the
more mundane LA hard rock influences overwhelm the sound.

This track is not terrible, but neither does it resolve into anything
particularly great. Yes, they've worked hard to find more focus, but
ultimately, it's stuck between a rock and a hard place: it's a great
instrumental unit slumming it.

'All Through The Night' (Shulman, Shulman, Minnear)
This song about the common man working to the clock and only
finding his brief blast of freedom at night is somewhat ironic, as the
band sound like they're playing to rule. Gary's multi-tracked heavy
chording and guitar hero riffing dominates, and the simple-minded
construction of the chorus is clearly geared towards the sing-along
crowd. This is by-the-book stuff.

'Shadows On The Street' (Shulman, Shulman, Minnear)
But just when you're thinking the whole album will be along the same
lines, here comes Kerry's one vocal turn on a lovely ballad, which captures
a reflective moment at the breaking of the day, as the thrall of the night
gives way to the industry of the working day. The song is based around
acoustic piano arpeggiations with traces of string synthesiser and some
bass chording. However, it shoe-horns Kerry's rarefied vocals into a more
conventional style through multitracking and a power ballad chorus. What
would come across as fairly ordinary on a great Gentle Giant album feels
like a bona fide classic in *Civilian's* reduced circumstances.

'Number One' (Shulman, Shulman, Minnear)
A lyrical broadside against someone who's slovenly and taking
advantage of all the protagonist's hard work, 'Number One' is a distant
relation to those songs about going their own way, including 'Funny
Ways' and 'Way Of Life'. But musically… oh dear. There's a nice swagger
to the drums, but this is play-by-numbers commercial rock/pop with the
group essentially aping the moves of then-successful American groups.

'Underground' (Shulman, Shulman, Minnear)

With simple lyrics describing an underground train station, and a beginning featuring the clattering and squealing of a train as it comes to a stop, 'Underground' has a train-on-tracks-like groove. It's not hard to imagine this released and expanded on a twelve-inch dance single, as its rhythmic style, choppy guitar and synthesizer sound isn't so far removed from the type of New Wave dance music in vogue in 1980. Despite its ordinary lyrics, the music hints at a path the group could have taken as Afro-American grooves started to permeate popular culture. But that road would have been as unlikely as commercial hard rock to play on the group's real strengths.

'I Am A Camera' (Shulman, Shulman, Minnear)

The lyrics of 'I Am A Camera' are oddly prescient, given the level of surveillance we exist under in the 21st century, but the tune makes it sound like a celebration rather than a warning. There's a tiny hint of Gentle Giant in the ascending motif, but that's the one stand-out feature. However, Derek's voice is well suited to this new power-pop direction, as it has the gravitas to carry the power chords and propulsive rhythms and fuses well with the vocal multi-tracking.

'Inside Out' (Shulman, Shulman, Minnear)

Lyrically, probably the most interesting song on *Civilian*, 'Inside Out' is the vaguely disturbing picture of a mentally disturbed individual who is losing all sense of self as he falls into the abyss. There's a genuine sense of danger and need in this intensely moody song, which provides one of the few near-great moments on an album with too few to mention.

It's the kind of song Roger Waters might have been proud to write, and it's fair to say that there are echoes of Pink Floyd here, but in many ways, the song harks back to the psychedelic era in its relentless building repetitions and almost hallucinogenic vocal harmonies.

'It's Not Imagination' (Shulman, Shulman, Minnear)

And then, it's back to earth with a thud on the last Gentle Giant track, sort of. For a song about worrying hidden messages in modern media, the relentlessly thudding commercial rock of 'It's Not Imagination' hardly conveys the idea. As with the album's opening song, 'Convenience (Clean And Easy)', the song is a comment on consumer society featuring Kerry's chunky, new wave-style, Devo-like synthesizer and almost metal-like riffing, and it's horrible.

But that's not quite all. Did Gentle Giant know that this was to be their last album? It would seem so, given by the fragment that appears right at the end – colloquially known as 'That's... All... There... Is' – which splices very short samples of their songs together. Just to confuse matters, however, this fragment doesn't appear on every version of the vinyl or CD, nor does it appear on streaming or online versions.

Odds and Sods

Under Construction

Unlike the compilations simply taken from existing albums, *Under Construction* (1997) is an essential collection for dedicated fans, as it brings together over two CDs an array of demos, outtakes and unreleased material. The first disc is subtitled 'Entirely Unreleased Material' and apart from the revelation of hearing completely unheard compositions, it also includes a few live cuts, and nine minutes and 18 seconds of isolated instrumentation. It's instructive to hear the first four songs recorded by the group in 1970, which are vastly different to the style of their first album, recorded just a few months later. It's hard to reconcile these songs with what the group became. Clearly, the group sound and ethos evolved at a blazing fast speed. But in 'Hometown Special' you can at least hear their vocal harmonies blossoming, although the music style is more like the kind of organ-drenched blues numbers with which Deep Purple are associated.

Other notable inclusions: the entertaining synthesizer/guitar duel that constitutes the music written for an aborted Robin Hood soundtrack; six minutes and 28 seconds-worth of guitar doodles in search of song ideas; Ray's mad violin solo on the nine minutes and 49 seconds of 'Timing' from one of the 1976 live shows from which *Playing The Fool* was taken; and a John Weathers song that displays a marked social conscience, 'You Haven't A Chance.'

The various demos on Disc 2 are self-explanatory, but let's have a detailed look at Disc 1 and its otherwise unreleased material:

'Radio Bit'

This is exactly what the title suggests: simply, Gentle Giant being introduced on the group's first radio exposure on 17 August 1970. Scratchy and very short, it's not clear what the group performed on this date, as the studio version of 'Freedoms Child' wasn't cut for another two weeks.

'Freedoms Child'

Gentle Giant fans listening to this for the first time will be floored at how different it is from the group's music just a few months later on their debut album. Those acquainted with the Simon Dupree And The Big Sound compilation, *Part Of My Past*, however, will hear the evolution.

'Freedoms Child' is, in many ways, very similar to the – largely unreleased in its day – flowery pop the Shulman brothers' previous group created in its last year or so. There are differences, however: the approach is less slick and Ray's prominent violin, together with Phil's plaintive vocals, gives it a folksy, elegiac feeling that imbues it with a certain down-home charm. It's instructive to compare this with the original demo of the song on disc two, which was recorded in 1968 by Kerry Minnear – who composed the piece – with a different set of musicians. The demo is muddled and ordinary.

'Hometown Special'
Recorded at the same session on sixteen tracks at Trident Studios on 29 August 1970, the style is utterly different from that of 'Freedoms Child'. A smouldering soul-drenched boogie on which organ is the lead instrument, it's of interest primarily because of the fairly elaborate harmony vocals where – in anticipation of the group's later complex a cappella work – there's a 'relay/echo' effect. The mid-section becomes an excuse for a fruity, blues-based solo by Gary, while the band's vamp could have seen them mistaken, once again, for Deep Purple.

'Weekend Cowboy'
Like 'Bringing Me Down' and 'Nothing At All', 'Weekend Cowboy' was recorded months before 'Freedoms Child' and 'Hometown Special'. In fact, these are Gentle Giant's first-ever recording sessions, recorded at Philips Studios on 23 February 1970.

'Weekend Cowboy' initially seems even less like the Gentle Giant we know and love than those two slightly later tunes. The difference is that a close listen reveals that there's a lot more going on here than the Caravan-styled, sweetly satirical take on hippy culture that at first hits you. In fact, they use a technique that Gentle Giant used extensively later on: two separate lead vocalists on different parts of the song.

It begins with Phil's gentle vocals to an acoustic backing and uncharacteristic harmonica, but the chorus deflects to Derek's multi-tracked and much more assertive vocal attack. Another feature that's already in place is the sheer craft and ingenuity that sees the piece orchestrated with stately violin, trumpet lines and even the odd touch of Mellotron.

'Bringing Me Down'
Starting out with harmony vocals in a soup of Mellotron, 'Bringing Me

Down' then turns into a groovesome R&B number with one of Derek's more soul-drenched vocals. This song is definitely harking back to the Shulman brothers' past in Simon Dupree And The Big Sound, except that instrumentally, it's leagues beyond that group, with Kerry providing beautiful touches of Mellotron, fruity organ and a hint of mallets.

'Nothing At All'
An earlier version of a classic track from the first album, 'Nothing At All' (all 8:23 of it) already has that faux-'Stairway To Heaven' guitar figure, but differs quite substantially in other ways. Martin's drums sound like they're auditioning for some b-grade hotel lobby jazz gig, and while its structure is substantially in place, the gorgeous harmonies aren't nearly as fulsome or well-developed, and it simply isn't the magic monster it would become on *Gentle Giant*. There is still a drum solo (yawn), though! Derek more or less gives up on singing the lines on this take of the song, which really belongs on the second, 'Demos and Outtakes' disc.

'Rondo – Playing The Game'
Really just 1:33 of doodles containing the memorable motif from 'Playing The Game'.

'DVS Guitars'
Recorded circa '75/'76, this is 6:28 of guitar fragments recorded by Derek and taken to the band as a contribution to the songwriting process. They're circular and nagging and entirely redolent of typical Gentle Giant structures.

'Robin Hood'
Recorded by Kerry and Ray for the battle scene of a Robin Hood movie they'd been asked to write demos for, this mere fragment (1:40) is intriguing, but with its eerie synth and dissonance, it's not surprising that the producers passed on the idea. What's bizarre about this is that the group would have been eminently capable of producing period-appropriate material for a Robin Hood film with the full group line-up, but instead chose this strange experiment. It's cool, though.

'Interview Whispers'
Simply the stereophonic 'whispers' that can be heard on 'Interview', Ray and Kerry in the left channel and Gary and Derek in the right. As it's

kind of hard to hear what's being whispered on the album, I guess this has some value for dedicated fans.

'Interview' / 'Timing'

Inexplicably included are live versions of 'Interview' and 'Timing' recorded on the *Playing The Fool* tour. As there was only one *Interview* song on that album, I guess there was some demand for this material to see the light of day in 1997, when *Under Construction* was released, but it hardly fits the theme of the set.

'Unreleased Civilian Track'

A muffled recording of a raw rehearsal for an unnamed song that never quite made it to *Civilian*. It's got a juicy, thrusting bass riff during the preamble, and a decent groove, but the main section cries out for vocals.

'You Haven't A Chance'

A John Weathers song about the plight of youth in Thatcher's England. It's a basic demo (just vocals, guitar and bass) that didn't make it onto *Civilian* for obvious reasons. It's not that it's bad, but it wouldn't have gelled with the slick, American-friendly sound of that album, and sounds nothing like Gentle Giant.

'Sample Archive'

One for all those DJs looking for cool sounds: 9:18 worth of isolated samples, including drum hits and moist Hammond grooves.
The second disc is entitled 'Demos And Outtakes' and is exactly that. It's inevitable that the versions here are not as good as the finished article, but it's a great insight into the band's working practices. In fact, at times it's a real fly-on-the-wall experience as the group, and sometimes individual members, literally figure out parts of songs that we, of course, have known and loved for years. The whole package is presented in a box with 28-page colour booklet, containing written reminiscences from the members.

Scraping The Barrel

It was almost as if the former members of Gentle Giant were setting their fans a challenge: 'You think *Under Construction* was hardcore? Well, then, try this!' While the second disc of that album gave us some insight into their writing and demoing processes, the four-disc *Scraping*

The Barrel box (note the ironic title), released in 2004, really went the whole hog. While this surfeit of material would have been downright confusing to anyone coming new to the group, it was hugely instructive for any serious student of their music.

The first disc presents material from their first seven albums, the second concentrates on their later albums, while the third collects bits and bobs of unreleased solo work. The fourth was a data disc, not a CD, and contained a wealth of MP3 files (many of them admittedly of poor sound quality), photos and PDFs of band memorabilia.

Once again, this is about as close as we'll ever get to being a fly on the wall, watching the band at work and hearing the creative juices flow. There are two main elements: band members chiselling away at writing and performing new songs, and isolated tracks. It's a pure joy being able to hear, for instance, the vocal mix of 'Pantagruel's Nativity' or 'Way Of Life' shorn of the vocals. In addition, there are jingles and outtakes and different versions. The big surprise is the third disc, and its 'new' material, most of which gathers together music worked on by Kerry after the dissolution of Gentle Giant. 'Home Again', for instance, is a gorgeous ballad recorded in 1984 which the others (minus Derek) added their parts to especially for the *Scraping The Barrel*.

It would take another book to explain this box set in detail, which contains 215 tracks and a mind-altering playing time of 748:14! Undoubtedly a treasure trove of delights for the avid GG admirer, our main point of interest is previously unreleased and new material, which languishes on Disc three. Before we get into that, however, it's important to point out that nothing on this disc sounds like Gentle Giant, or quite matches the group's fine standards. The fact that former members of the group could never aspire to Gentle Giant's greatness in their subsequent work is not surprising, given the almost supranatural way they worked together.

There are many similar examples of brilliant musicians/writers working wonders in the right collaborative situation, yet finding it impossible to find their musical mojo alone or in different contexts. One of the most startling is the case of The Doors. While guitarist Robbie Krieger wrote a number of that group's classic songs, after singer Jim Morrison died, Krieger never wrote another. The group's two albums without Morrison were fairly dire, and while Krieger's excellent guitar skills can be heard on many different albums over the decades, the songs just aren't there, and the various elements just don't quite coalesce.

As I discuss elsewhere in this book, perhaps Gentle Giant's key genius is the dedication they showed over their ten-year span to working together in a more-or-less democratic fashion. While one member may sometimes contribute the larger part of a composition, when that material goes into the collaborative pot, it becomes something bigger, brighter and beefier. It becomes the property of Gentle Giant and is all the better for it.

Could any of the members have gone on to stellar careers in music-making, either as solo artists or in a different musical groupings? We'll never know, but I would guess not. The fickle tide of fashion was against them, for starters. Kerry could certainly have composed beautiful soundtracks for Old England-themed motion pictures and documentaries, and as disc three of this set shows, Ray has more recently shown a late-blooming talent for soundtrack work. But there's a sense in all these tracks that there's either something missing or that things are not quite what they could be. Without the rest of the group to balance his musings, Kerry's solo work tends to sound a little trite and comfy. Within the setting of Gentle Giant, his more delicate and melodic ballad ideas were presented with an edge that's missing from his post-Gentle Giant work. Similarly, the post-punk/new wave sound of Gary and Ray's early 1980s project lacks the contrast and surprise of their previous band.

There are examples of 1970s progressive groups whose members went on to forge extraordinary bodies of work in the 1980s. Drummer Charles Hayward left Phil Manzanera's Quiet Sun to form the phenomenal This Heat, while Henry Cow evolved into Art Bears. But these bands/individuals belong to the avant-garde end of the progressive rock spectrum, and as we know, Gentle Giant had made the decision to try and get commercial traction by watering down their sound in 1977, with the deeply flawed *The Missing Piece*. It could be argued that the result would be a slippery slope with few of the commercial benefits hoped for and a loss in musical credibility from which they could never quite recover.

'Home Again'

The first eleven songs on disc 3 are all Kerry Minnear originals recorded after Gentle Giant dissolved.

'Home Again' is a poignant piece, even if it comes across as a bit cloying and sentimental. It's easy to imagine that the lyrics might relate to his time with the band and where he's at now:

I've been around this world/And I've seen so many wonderous things. But now's the time in my life/When I need to rest… There was a time when ambition spurred my thoughts/And in that time I can say that I really found contentment. But now I find it matters not/I'm back, back where I belong.

Like 'Moog Fugue' and 'Move Over', featuring Kerry with John, Ray and Phil making contributions, it's as close to a reunited Gentle Giant lineup as we may ever see, but of course, sounds nothing like them.

'Moog Fugue'

This is exactly what you imagine a keyboardist with a classical background might concoct: a Moog-based instrumental piece that starts out with fruity synth layering but which is eventually joined by drums, guitar (phoned in by Gary) and multiple overdubbed keyboards. It almost swings.

'Move Over'

Again featuring 'those other guys', 'Move Over' sees Kerry attempting a very middle of the road pop/rock song. The lyrics, forged by John, critique someone's motives: 'Move over/let me breathe.' It certainly shows Kerry's substantial skills at fashioning a composition, but the song demands a stronger vocalist. As Kerry explains in the liner notes to *Scraping The Barrel*, he wrote this song intending to sell it to Cliff Richard.

'Really Don't Know'

The next five tracks are Kerry's 'Chrysalis demos' from 1983. The story goes that Gentle Giant's Chrysalis contract demanded one more album. As they'd broken up, Kerry worked up these demos, which the label promptly rejected. Consequently, the band members were released from the contract. As a whole, these demos are simply not convincing, and are so stylistically diverse that they appear to be created to show his diversity rather than any overall musical personality. What's likely – as with 'Move Over' – is that Kerry was writing material with a view to finding popular artists to cover his compositions.

'Really Don't Know' is easily the best of the bunch, and it would have made a very entertaining single in an era where such characterful novelties were consumed with relish (think Ian Dury or Madness or Squeeze). 'I've got no real amazing talent/When I'm lying in bed I lose my balance/The tax return is quite a challenge/And I burn my nose when I'm lighting fag ends,' go the lyrics, which were written by Andy Read. And then the weary, laconic chorus: 'I really don't know, I really don't care/It really doesn't make a scrap of difference.' The keyboard sound – lightly funky synth-pop – is very much of its era, but remains palatable.

'Heaven's Tears'
Another 1983 Chrysalis demo, 'Heaven's Tears' has '80s keyboards and a bendy guitar sound redolent of Mark Knopfler. Unfortunately, Kerry's voice sounds rather weak on this material, and the ballad itself reeks of cliché.

'Flower Arranging'
Another Chrysalis demo on which Kerry's light and happy vocal just isn't strong enough to make it work. There's some bouncy synth on 'Peruvian flute setting' on this Latin-inspired piece. Phil Thomson contributes the lyric.

'Living In A Restaurant'
For a 1980s synth/keyboards fetishist, 'Living In A Restaurant' and 'You Make Me Very Happy' will hold a certain allure, but for the rest of us? Hmm. The second-to-last Chrysalis demo is fashioned like a children's song. A child asks him, 'What's it like living in a restaurant?' and he thinks about his friends with their fancy cars and houses. Kerry wrote the lyrics, which were 'about the strange effect distance has on social conscience.'

'You Make Me Very Happy'
The last of the Chrysalis demos is a somewhat plodding, very 1980s synth-pop song. As with 'Really Don't Know', Kerry aims for an almost Ian Dury comedic impact on the verse before the sappy, anthemic chorus, which consists pretty much of the song's title.

'Get Out Of My Way'
And here begins the religious content. Supposedly more Kerry, but it's not specified as to which era it pertains, or who's on it. This is standard raunchy rock'n'roll fodder with a Jesus message and Kerry (if it is indeed him singing) is trying to sing to style. The result is ordinary, and where are the keyboards? 'Whoa baby, my head fell off/I've never

felt this power of love.' But then: 'Get outta my way/Get outta my way/I want to see Jesus and you're standing in my way.'

'Wisdom Was Calling'
This has nice chattering synths, and a layered vocal that's recognisably Kerry. But it's an odd mishmash, and its overtly Christian message isn't easy to swallow. Still, 'Wisdom Was Calling' is a jaunty wee thing and likable enough.

'Good Christian Men Rejoice'
Kerry's voice is nicely layered and suits the material on 'Good Christian Men Rejoice', which is of course, overtly religious. The last of the Kerry tracks has Gentle Giant sounding keyboards and even a style with more than a strand of medievalism about it. Excerpted from The Reapers' *Christmas Joy* cassette.

'HavaNagila'
This is the first of two songs by Simon Dupree And The Big Sound that inexplicably failed to make the cut on the *Part Of My Past* compilation. This one a rather odd choice for a single, as it's a rendering of the old Israeli folk song. It sounds like they couldn't find the master tape, as it's noticeably thin in sonics. The story goes that the group performed this live to a rousing reception, so their manager suggested that they record it – at which point they realised that it was rather a silly idea.

'Homeland'
A very pleasant and rather melancholy instrumental ballad by Simon Dupree And The Big Sound featuring acoustic guitar, organ, piano, drums and violin. It was the proposed B-side to 'HavaNagila'.

'Burn My Working Clothes'
The bare bones of a song, really, this bluesy 1982 John Weathers track is a raw demo with guitar and bass (playing guitar-like notes) but no drums, and no voice. It was recorded properly with lyrics/vocals by Welsh band Man (with John on drums) fourteen years later.

'On Safari'
The following three songs are credited to Shout, a short-lived duo of Gary Green and Ray Shulman that was formed shortly after the demise of Gentle Giant. The story goes that the project didn't last because Gary

had moved to America, which made working together in pre-digital times next to impossible. 'On Safari' finds Kerry imploring his young daughter, Sally (who has since gone on to a musical career in her own right), to say the name of the song – very cute – then it's into a heavily percussive rock song with keys on 'flute' setting. Kerry is there because it's being recorded in his home studio. This piece was created as an instrumental theme for a children's TV show and is both happy and brief.

'Starting Line' (Demo)
The A-side of Shout's only single, 'Starting Line' was released in 1980 and this demo version (the single version remains in the vault) is a creditable slice of post-punk/new wave. It has cross-picked and echoed guitars and a sound reminiscent of early 1980s Psychedelic Furs or The Cure. Gary performs on guitar and drums while Ray plays bass and guitar. The b-side, 'Walk Don't Talk', also remains in the vault.

'Running Away' (Demo)
'Running Away' is very propulsive and again the sound is pure post-punk with a vocal that sounds like early Cure. As in 'Starting Line', the vocals seem to be about not fitting in and alienation.

'Our World'
This is Gary Green circa 1991. Featuring both picked guitar parts and sheets of sound, this piece has a nice motif but the vocals are weak. It's a theme-like piece with jangly guitars that inevitably conjure images of Robert Fripp's League Of Crafty Guitars.

'Back To The Front'
This is Gary again on a piece with a humping beat, bass guitar riff... and weak vocals. The guitar work is excellent, but...

'Prehistoric Boss Level'
A Ray Shulman project that finds him composing for computer games, and it has that kind of super-visual, cinematic feel to it – orchestral and mysterious and very 'folie' (SFX).

'Volcano'
Ditto this piece, which is more moody and reticent with snares and pizzicato violins, and does a great job of drumming up the kind of musical-visual imagery one expects from cinema or computer games.

Memories Of Old Days

And just to confuse matters, *Memories Of Old Days* (2013) is yet another box of rehearsals, demos, live songs and miscellaneous odds and sods. Subtitled 'A Compendium Of Curios, Bootlegs, Live Tracks, Rehearsals And Demos 1975-1980', it's considerably less necessary than the first box, and in fact, there is rather a lot of duplication. I guess the reasoning was that the data disc on *Scraping The Barrel* would become inaccessible over time with the march of technology, and the first two discs here are taken from that disc.

The first disc features the usual variety of studio excerpts – including a rather tedious seventeen minutes of Kerry working on 'I Lost My Head' – and is interjected by some seemingly randomly-selected live material. The second disc consists entirely of tour rehearsals from 1977. Interest in these performances will depend on one's tolerance for *The Missing Link*-period material, although there are a few back-catalogue selections. The third disc contains six rehearsals/studio extracts and a further eleven from a live show in Cleveland, the same show previously featured on a truncated version on the *Missing Face* CD. The fourth disc is audio of the twelve-song 1978 BBC Sight and Sound Concert, which is fine except that it duplicates the CD included with the DVD of the same gig. It also includes five demos from *Scraping The Barrel*.

Finally, disc 5 features a couple of rehearsals (from *Scraping The Barrel*, again) and selections from two 1980 gigs, one at New Haven and the other their last-ever concert at The Roxy, which is a duplication of the *Last Steps* CD. While *Scraping The Barrel* is packed full of goodies, *Memories Of Old Days* really does feel like it's scraping the barrel, and it's a bit sad for completists that there's so much duplication.

Compilations and Videos

If ever there was a group for whom compilations drawn from their albums were irrelevant, it's Gentle Giant. They were an 'album group', and most of those albums were conceptual in nature, and therefore, designed to be listened to from beginning to end. They've been better served by a small but cherishable number of compilations drawn from demos, unreleased songs, and radio sessions. And their two DVDs give an essential perspective on the members and the working group.

Giant Steps

While *Giant Steps*, released in 1976, is a fair summation of the group's mighty Vertigo years and contains many of their finest songs over its four sides, it's not a patch on hearing the albums from whence they came, in the order in which they were intended. To confuse matters, when the album was reissued on double CD in 2012 by Talking Elephant, 'The Face' and 'The Runaway' were omitted in favour of five new tracks, 'Black Cat', 'Dog's Life', 'The Queen', 'Working All Day' and 'Wreck'.

Pretentious – For The Sake Of It

Only one year later, 1977, and Vertigo were raking it in again with yet another double LP compilation drawn from the group's years with the label. With only 'The Runaway' appearing on both collections, if nothing else it shows just what a wealth of great material the label had at its disposal.

Champions Of Rock

A Dutch-made CD from 1996 that compiles tracks from *Free Hand* through to *Giant For A Day*, but missing their last album, *Civilian*. Some fans initially claimed that these were different mixes, but it turned out that they were simply mastered at the wrong speed. Avoid.

Edge Of Twilight

Yet another album – a 1996 double CD – that draws mostly from the Vertigo years, but for some reason omits *In A Glass House* and adds selections from *The Power And The Glory*. It's compiled with respect by mega-GG fan Dan Barrett, who made sure that the songs were nicely remastered, and even fixed the recurrent glitch on 'Acquiring The Taste' that occurs on most CD versions. It also includes thoughtful and well-informed liner notes.

Giant On The Box

Given Gentle Giant's relatively short lifespan, footage of the band is on the slim side, which makes both *Giant On The Box* and *GG At The GG – Sight and Sound In Concert* the more important and necessary acquisitions.

Giant On The Box (2005), the 'deluxe edition' of which includes a bonus CD, will be a revelation to any fan who is familiar with the group's recorded work but never got the opportunity to catch them live at their peak. The first section captures them performing eight songs to a captive audience in a Brussels film studio in 1974, and it's a veritable 'best of' with muscular renditions of 'Cogs In Cogs', 'Proclamation', 'Funny Ways', 'The Runaway', 'Experience', the *Octopus* medley, 'Advent Of Panurge' and 'So Sincere'. Although they were already seasoned performers by '74, they still look comparatively young and fresh-faced, and it's interesting to note their apparel, including Kerry's fancy silk get-up, Derek's Indian-style dhoti and Ray's knave costume.

The camera work is rudimentary and tends to view the band from the right, which means there are many more great shots of Kerry at his keyboards or vibraphone or cello and John bashing the hell out of those drums than there are close-ups of Gary and his guitar wizardry. Whatever intricacies are lost in comparison to the recordings are made up for by exuberance and sheer energy, and it's a great opportunity to see the famed instrument swapping in action. During 'The Runaway' (with Derek on sax!) Kerry plays a wild keyboard solo before returning to his favoured instrument, the clavinet. Later, on the *Octopus* medley, Kerry briefly 'does an Emerson' by playing several keyboards simultaneously and squeezing out squiggly, Wakemanesque Moog lines.

The 50-minute Brussels segment ends with 'So Sincere', which features the group all going for it on various percussion instruments. Primitively shot and miked by today's standards, it's a great exposition of the group's unpretentious balls-and-all approach to live performance.

Szene '74 is a 3:08 minute fragment filmed during that year's European tour, while the four songs recorded at Long Beach in '75 (30:47) replicates 'Experience', the *Octopus* medley, 'Advent Of Panurge' and 'Funny Ways' from the Brussels date. The big difference is the onstage garb, which is much less frilly. Interestingly, they fluff the start of 'Funny Ways', stop it, introduce it again and have another go. Presumably, only the second take was used when it was broadcast. This song is of special interest mainly because Kerry goes apeshit on vibes.

Baroque and Roll is a short black and white film from Italian television thought to have been recorded in '76, in which the group sit around answering questions between snatches of performance. The problem is that their answers have Italian voice-overs.

In addition, there's a 2005 music television interview with Derek to promote the 35th anniversary CD reissues that's only mildly interesting, due to the DJ's overbearing blabber, as well as a selection of band photographs.

The bonus CD contains both the Brussels and Long Beach performances.

GG At The GG – Sight and Sound In Concert

Easily the lesser of the two Gentle Giant DVDs, its main event is the 1978 concert they performed for the BBC's *Sight and Sound* TV show.

This 60-minute gig comes over as a little odd, which is easily explained by the circumstances. The group wasn't exactly hot news in the post-punk environment of the time, so in the first instance, it's rather bizarre that they were chosen for a TV gig that would normally go to a band that was considered on the boil. On top of that, by this time they were virtually invisible in the UK. Indeed, this would be their last-ever onstage appearance in England.

But perhaps strangest of all was that the audience – which seems to fill just a small proportion of the seating in Golders Green Hippodrome, London – was chosen at random and had no idea whose concert they were going to. For some audience members being assailed and assaulted musically by Gentle Giant must have been quite a shock!

The group performs 12 songs and prove – again! – that they're still one of the most adept, interesting and innovative bands on the scene. Unfortunately, the show was performed on the heels of *The Missing Piece*, and several of its worst songs get an airing, including the risible punk-baiting 'Betcha Thought We Couldn't Do It'. This song, ironically, elicits the most enthusiastic response from the crowd and the set also includes the cod-funk 'Mountain Time'. The sound quality is good, and their renditions of 'Free Hand', 'Playing The Game' and 'Funny Ways' are uniformly great, but it's all somewhat blighted by then-recent songs like 'Two Weeks In Spain' and the pseudo-Genesis 'I'm Turning Around', which comes across as laboured and over-long. Kerry's keyboards are looking particularly beaten-up – perhaps an indication that they weren't expecting to land this prestige television gig. Or perhaps the whole rig was hired!

The best thing about the DVD is the commentary from the group members, a jovial session in which they make some interesting observations. Derek is particularly scathing about his white boiler suit (rightly so!) and he states outright that he hates 'Betcha Thought We Couldn't Do It' and doesn't know what they were trying to do with 'Mountain Time'. It's a delight to hear the five members together and the inevitable repartee that results.

The DVD is filled out with six video clips shot to promote *Interview* (1976) and *Giant For A Day* (1978). These are simple studio shoots in London and Los Angeles respectively, and they're uniformly average. Still, it's voyeuristically fascinating to see the group try their hand at promotional clips in these pre-MTV days.

Finally, there's yet another version of the *Octopus* medley from the *Old Grey Whistle Test* and a fragment of handheld Super 8 footage, and two galleries taken from Gary's photo collection. Hardcore fans will be intrigued by the menu music, which was written by Kerry using John's drum fills taken from the multi-tracks.

Live Albums

The first thing any self-proclaimed 'real' fan of Gentle Giant will point out is that you haven't really heard the band unless you've experienced them in concert. This news is irrelevant for the many who either lived somewhere the band never toured or discovered the group after they disbanded, but it's tremendous solace for those who have seen them in concert and have only fading memories to remind them of Gentle Giant's live splendiferousness.

Unfortunately, live albums tend to fall way short of capturing the essence of a group, and that was especially true in the 1970s when recording technology was comparatively primitive. For starters, live performances in the '70s were often plagued with gear malfunction, PA issues, unintentional feedback and poor sound balance between instruments. Recording a gig 'properly' meant the delicate task of combining the up-close desk recording with a separate 'atmosphere' recording of crowd noise.

While live recordings of Gentle Giant are plentiful, the more numerous and better-recorded ones are largely from 1975 and later, and the vast majority of them are audience recordings (some dweeb with a cassette recorder) with poor fidelity, and therefore only really of historical interest. That's why the main course for prospective Gentle Giant fans is still the peak-years studio albums, regardless of the fact that the excitement and energy of live performance is lacking. That's also why the best Gentle Giant live albums are placed right at the beginning of this section, and they're then listed in (more or less) descending order of interest. Nothing will change the fact that indisputably, *Playing The Fool* is one of the greatest live albums of all time, and that every other live release is merely a footnote in comparison.

There are those, of course, who have to have it all – even bootlegs of dire quality. And fair enough. While a fan like myself is primarily interested in the best quality fidelity with which to enjoy the music, there's also a different kind of fan who will need to hear every single live recording and have it catalogued in exact sequence. It takes all kinds!While the reviews below are indicative, it's not an exhaustive list of every live album. By and large, I've concentrated on official releases, many of which started out as bootlegs but have since been reissued by the band. New live recordings are turning up with more frequency as interest in Gentle Giant picks up, and some fans are even releasing albums-worth of previously unheard material exclusively on YouTube.

The recently released, mammoth box set, *Unburied Treasure*, features a further fifteen live CDs, the first five being of especial interest as they capture the band in rare 1972 and 1973 performances. Several of these, however, have previously appeared (see reviews below). These CDs are: *Essen 1972, New Orleans 1972, Hollywood Bowl 1972, Vicenza 1973, Torino 1973, Munster 1974, St Gallen 1974, Cleveland Agora 1975, Basel 1975, Dusseldorf 1976, Brussels 1976, Munich 1976, Paris 1976, Chester 1977* and *Roxy 1980*.

Note: Even though *Playing The Fool* isn't a studio album, this book includes it in the main album reviews section for sequential reasons.

Live At The Bicentennial

Recorded earlier the same year as *Playing The Fool, Live At The Bicentennial* provides further insight on the *In'terview* tour.Not released officially until 2014, this double CD captures the group performing to an American audience the night before Independence Day in 1976.

Taped by a local radio station, the sound quality is surprisingly rich, but the sonic balance isn't as well defined as *Playing The Fool*, and there's some distortion.

A chance to hear 'Timing' (here stretched out to 13:34 with some wild violin soloing from Ray) and 'Give It Back' from *In'terview*, it's a necessary purchase for dedicated fans. Note that this is a sonically improved version of the 'grey area' *Interview In Concert* release.

In Concert/Out Of The Fire: The BBC Concerts From 1973 and 1978

Originally only available in a pressing of 50 for radio play and hugely collectable, this 1978 BBC Radio *In Concert* session, released on CD in 1994, is the same Hippodrome, Golders Green Sight and Sound performance subsequently released on *GG At The GG*. Consequently, it's hampered by the same set-list issues, as it gives priority to some of the worst songs from *The Missing Piece*, including 'Mountain Time' and 'Betcha Thought We Couldn't Do It.' At least on this audio-only disc, we don't have to look at Derek's embarrassing white boiler suit. The sound quality is excellent.

Out Of The Fire, released in 1998, is an expanded 2-CD set featuring an additional BBC concert from 1973 including four highlights from that era: 'Way Of Life', 'Funny Ways', 'Nothing At All' and 'Excerpts From Octopus'. The version of *In Concert* is preferable to the original CD as it includes 'Funny Ways' and has the songs in the right order.

Out Of The Woods: The BBC Sessions/Totally Out Of The Woods: The BBC Sessions

Originally released on CD in 1996, *Out Of The Woods* was effectively made redundant by the issue of *Totally Out Of The Woods* in 2000, which expands it to double-album length, although only adds an extra twenty minutes. The additions comprise a bit of DJ banter, a 1973 session that comprises 'Way Of Life', 'The Runaway', 'The Advent Of Panurge' and a 'live demo' of 'Free Hand'.

It's arguable as to whether a band's BBC Sessions can be considered 'live', as there is no audience. Nevertheless, the whole idea was live-in-studio, and *Totally Out Of The Woods* compiles several sessions and eras of the many they did for the BBC over the years – some of which are now lost to time and the BBC's tendency to erase old tapes.

BBC sessions never shine up as vividly as the official recordings, but they're important for completists, as they give the fan a chance to glimpse the band in a more informal studio setting where they don't have the time to get too fancy, as only a few hours is allowed for post-production. As Gary writes in the liner notes, the sessions were always a challenge as the BBC studios were ancient and the layers of their music had to be squeezed onto fewer tracks.

Totally Out Of The Woods contains the first two (of three) tracks recorded for the band's first session, as well as their seventh, eighth, tenth[th] and eleventh[th] (and last) session. Overall, it's great to hear the band 'in the raw' though and experience the progress they made from 1970 to 1975.

'City Hermit'

For many, the very first song, non-album 1970 track 'City Hermit', will be the most interesting moment, as it's like Gentle Giant channelling Deep Purple. For many years this was one of the rarest of the group's tracks and a poor quality live version circulated on cassette, so it's a revelation to hear a studio recording. Actually, it sounds great: big, warm and vibrant, and it chugs along nicely for 4:47. Those expecting even a semblance of the real Gentle Giant sound might be disappointed, however. While its bluesy, organ-drenched sound is great and shows Kerry in a slightly different light, there's little hint of the complexity or the specific characteristics that would come to define the group.

The Last Steps

As the title suggests, this is a recording of Gentle Giant's final concert at the Roxy in Los Angeles, California, from June 16, 1980, the CD of which was first released in 1996 and reissued in 2003 with slightly clearer sound. It's a rough and ready recording with frequent drop-outs and mixing problems with Gary's guitar inaudible at times. But the show captures the almost desperate urgency of a band who've decided to call it a day and are giving their all, on what they know is their last shot.

The only sour note is the song selection itself, which includes some of the weaker, later numbers like 'All Through The Night' and 'Giant For A Day' where they could almost be any hard rocking AOR band. Happily, however, they run through energetic versions of 'Free Hand', 'Knots', and 'The Advent Of Panurge'. While *The Last Steps* is only for hardcore fans, and shows just how much of the band's character has been sacrificed in an attempt to meet the market, it also confirms that at the time of their dissolution, Gentle Giant were still a superb, dynamic live proposition.

King Biscuit Flower Hour Presents Gentle Giant
Recorded on January 18, 1975, at the Academy Of Music in New York and released on CD in 1998, this 45-minute, seven-song album is one of many live releases from the radio show *King Biscuit Flower Hour*. The audio quality is decent, but as can be expected of this kind of thing, it stops short of being a full show, and some of the pieces are truncated due to the time constraints of radio.

While ultimately, nothing replaces *Playing The Fool* as the ultimate live example of the group, these performances ('Proclamation', 'Funny Ways', 'The Runaway', 'Experience', 'So Sincere', 'Knots', 'The Advent Of Panurge') from the *Power And The Glory* tour are pretty spectacular.

Live Rome 1974
A 'grey area' CD originally released as *Giant Steps Forward* in 1994 and reissued as *Live Rome 1974* in 1998, this 70-minute album starts out with a lot of background noise and there's a (mercifully, fairly brief) burst of horrible ringing noise during 'Cogs In Cogs' as well. Another recording anomaly is that Gary's guitar is mixed so low that it sometimes disappears entirely. Despite the recording imperfections, however – some of which are hugely offputting – the performances themselves are typically superb.

Overall, the audio is like an average desk-recorded bootleg, while the band obviously haven't been consulted. The cover lacks production

credits and carelessly uses photos from different periods of Gentle
Giant's career. My advice is to choose the King Biscuit Hour CD instead,
as it was recorded mere months later on the same tour (*The Power And
The Glory*).

In A Palesport House
Well, this really is scraping the barrel! Originally released as a bootleg
in 1998, its 'official' release was in 2001, but this is still a crummy-
sounding recording that is, accordingly, hard to enjoy. Only the diehards
who must own every concert fragment will need this, which admittedly
does capture them on one of their less-recorded tours in support of *In
A Glass House* in 1973.

Although the cover claims it was recorded in Rome on January 3, it's
actually the same October 19 performance included on the data disc of
Scraping The Barrel, natch. And to make matters even more confusing,
the last two tracks are from the 1974 Longbeach ABC In Concert.

Artistically Cryme
A 2-CD set with a running time of one hour and 47 minutes, like *In
A Palesport House*, this started its life as a bootleg in 2000 and was
reissued in 2002. You've really got to ask why they bothered with an
audience recording that's of such poor audio fidelity. Recorded at Lund,
Sweden on September 19, 1976, it's really of little use to anyone but a
dedicated Gentle Giant archaeologist.

Endless Life
Two hours and 13 minutes on two compact discs and a near-repeat
of *Artistically Cryme*: originally released as a bootleg in 2001, it was
'officially' (meaning that the former members of Gentle Giant now
received the royalties/proceeds) released in 2002. Recorded in New
York on October 3, 1975, and Berkley on October 28, it's another
audience recording that's lacking in depth or definition, and there are
far better in concert examples of Gentle Giant at this time.

The Missing Face
Yet another album that started life as a bootleg, this 2001 release was
recorded in Cleveland in November 1977 and as expected, includes
then-new material from *The Missing Piece* like 'Betcha Thought We
Couldn't Do It' and 'Two Weeks In Spain'. Sound quality is below
average.

Prologue

Are you bored yet? This is another 2-CD 'grey area' set from 2001 that captures Gentle Giant primarily on their *In A Glass House* tour, recorded in Muenster on April 5, 1974, but adds on songs recorded in Philadelphia on October 10, 1975

It's hard going because of the very average-sounding bootleg-quality audience recording, complete with momentary equipment irruptions and annoyingly inappropriate audience noise close to the microphone. And it's mono, of course.

Playing The Cleveland

Another bootleg that was given an 'official' release in 2005, tracks one to six were recorded in Cleveland on January 27, 1975, while the last two songs ('Cogs In Cogs, 'The Runaway/Experience') are of unknown provenance. Once again, poor audio mars one's listening pleasure, and there are plenty of superior live examples of the band around this time.

Live In New York 1975

Apparently, an 'official' album recorded on October 7, 1975 and released on CD in 2005. Featuring just six tracks, and very similar to *Endless Life* which was recorded just days earlier, it's another bootleg-style recording that will only be of interest to GG archaeologists and necrophiliacs.

Live In Santa Monica 1975

Originally released as a bootleg in 2001 and reissued as an 'official' album in 2005, information is scant about this recording from the *Free Hand* tour, but it's another poor quality audience recording of containing seven songs. Ditto the above warnings.

Live In Stockholm '75

The audio is crystal clear on this official live CD, licensed to Gentle Giant by Swedish Radio. Recorded in Stockholm on November 12, 1975, and released in 2009, it captures the band in fine form during one of the peaks of its career and leaves all the other 'grey area' bootleg-style releases in the dust.

The CD booklet features live pics and reminiscences by the band members. In other words, the package has been put together with love and care – unlike those shoddy bootleg-style albums above.

King Alfred's College Winchester

Recorded on February 12, 1971 on cassette, this is a bootleg-quality release on Alucard, Gentle Giant's label with a few mid-song glitches where the song is interrupted by the need to turn over the tape.

Normally, I would warn fans off exploring a release of such compromised audio fidelity, but this is the earliest known recording of the band in concert. As such, it's an incredible insight into where they were at musically only seven weeks after the release of the debut album, *Gentle Giant*. What's more, *King Alfred's College Winchester* features obscure tracks like 'Hometown Special' and 'City Hermit', studio versions of which first appeared on *Under Construction*. It would have been reasonable to assume that these songs never made it to their live repertoire, given the progress Gentle Giant made between their first clutch of compositions and those that made the cut on *Gentle Giant*. Another oddity is the final song, 'Peel Off The Paint', which features the same lyrics as 'Peel The Paint' (*Three Friends*) but completely different music!

It's also instructive to hear the rather low-key way they chat away to an audience that claps politely rather than especially enthusiastically. Despite the dull, muted sound quality, there's almost no audience noise during songs, which is a major bonus, and the performances – though very different to the martial discipline and manic energy of mid-period gigs – are a real treat.

Reissues/Remasters

Gentle Giant were, for a long time, poorly served by reissues. Where most of their progressive rock contemporaries stayed with their labels over the long term, Gentle Giant switched from Vertigo to Chrysalis in the mid-1970s. But if it was only that simple. For instance, the Vertigo albums were distributed by Columbia in the US, while the group's Chrysalis albums were on Capitol in America. Making matters much more complicated in the era of the compact disc, was the fact that the major labels with which they had been affiliated weren't interested in 'heritage' groups, resulting in the albums being leased out to a variety of small reissue labels in the '80s and '90s whose attention to detail left a lot to be desired.

Not only was the sound quality disappointing on many of the early issues, but some of the discs had errors. For instance, the German Line Records CD of *Gentle Giant* is strangely missing the synth riffs that are supposed to appear before 'Alucard' and 'Isn't It Quiet And Cold', along with other discrepancies. On several versions of the title tune from *Acquiring The Taste* the first two notes are bent out of shape. Ditto the Line Records reissue of *Octopus*, which contains minor defects that can be heard on headphones, and the Vertigo CD of the same album, which is notably compressed. The Line Records release of *Three Friends*, meanwhile, sounds like it was taken from a dilapidated master. And so it goes. Needless to say, these earlier CD issues also skimped on booklets, liners and replicating the original cover artwork.

Then in 2005, the group released three mastered 35th Anniversary Edition CDs on Derek's DRT label. These sounded a little better than previous iterations but were harsh-sounding, and there were notable omissions from the catalogue. The artwork was partially restored, but there were no liner notes, the cash instead being poured into pointless 35th Anniversary cardboard covers to slip over the jewel boxes.

While purportedly remastered editions of the missing titles appeared in 2011, fans are still waiting for definitive versions that restore the sound to its pristine glory. The 35th-anniversary edition of *In A Glass House* that's on the streaming services, for instance, features a worrying amount of hiss, feeding rumours that the multitracks for this pivotal album have been lost forever. Hopefully, the supposedly remastered albums in the *Unburied Treasures* box will get individual releases. Or better yet, that Steven Wilson will turn his attention to these for CD/Blu-ray sets that mimic the excellent *Octopus* and *The Power And The Glory* reissues.

It's inevitable that over the many reissues of reissues the labels have tempted fans by adding a few extra tracks. Accordingly, the 35th-anniversary series added several live tracks to each album. While it was great to hear live versions of tracks from the studio album, these were really surplus to requirements, and best featured on dedicated live releases.

I Lost My Head – The Chrysalis Years (1975-1980)
I Lost My Head is simply a bringing together of the Chrysalis label albums: *Free Hand, In'terview, The Missing Piece, Playing The Fool, Giant For A Day* and *Civilian*. Released in 2012, it bungs everything onto four CDs, so *In'terview* shares a CD with *The Missing Piece* and *Giant For A Day* shares a CD with *Civilian. Playing The Fool* (originally a double vinyl album) takes up one CD while a bunch of John Peel sessions and seven-inch mixes are added to *Free Hand*.

The only compelling reason to purchase this set is the remastering, which is superior to that of the 35th Anniversary CDs, and the first time that *Civilian* has been remastered.

Free Hand/Interview
Also in 2012, *Free Hand* and *In'terview* were released as a CD/DVD set. The DVD featured a previously unreleased quadraphonic mix (in DTS 96/24) and the albums featured sleeve-notes written by band members. The albums were also reissued on vinyl. This one is already out of print and hard to come by.

The Power And The Glory
Released in 2014, the first of the Gentle Giant Steven Wilson remixes was this perennially popular (with fans) album, and it's hard to think how they could further improve it. Released in a handsome foldout digipack, containing a glossy booklet with a selection of photos and liner notes by Sid Smith, the CD features the Steven Wilson mix of the album and a couple of bonus tracks in 'The Power And The Glory' (not featured on the original album) and an instrumental outtake of 'Aspirations'.

The Blu-ray disc, meanwhile, features Wilson's hi-res 5.1 surround mix of the album, as well as a hi-res stereo mix, the whole album *sans* vocals, and a flat transfer of the original 1974 studio mix – all with entertaining on-screen graphics. Wilson's mixes are faithful to the original album but bring out detail that had previously been obscured.

His surround sound mix is an opportunity for fans to hear a new degree of separation in the instrumentation that makes for a revelatory listening experience. It's a wonderful presentation of an equally wonderful album that reeks of love and attention to detail.

Octopus
Released in 2015, the second of the Gentle Giant Steven Wilson remixes was for *Octopus*, the 1972 album that remains a fan favourite. As with Wilson's remix job for *The Power And The Glory*, it's hard to imagine how it could be further improved. Like that album, *Octopus* is presented in a handsome foldout digipack containing a glossy booklet with a selection of photos and liner notes, this time round by GG scholar Anil Prasad.

The CD features the Steven Wilson mix of the album and a 1976 live performance of 'Excerpts From Octopus', presumably simply to provide context and compare the studio and live versions. The Blu-ray disc, meanwhile, features Wilson's hi-res 5.1 surround mix of the album, as well as a hi-res stereo mix, the whole album *sans* vocals, and a flat transfer of the original 1972 studio mix – all with entertaining on-screen graphics. Master reels of only five of the eight tracks could be found, so Wilson remastered the remaining tracks, along with creating virtual surround mixes using Penteo software. Regardless, Wilson has further improved on what was already a fine sounding album.

Three Piece Suite
Released in 2017, *Three Piece Suite* is a revelation to longtime fans, as these Steven Wilson remixes give a completely fresh perspective on recordings that many fans have only heard on a series of poorly mastered CD reissues over the years.

But, in a perfect world *Three Piece Suite* would be simply a stop-gap measure, as it's a compilation of the only multi-track recordings that have been found from the first three albums. Hopefully, in the fullness of time all the multitrack recordings will be found and *Gentle Giant*, *Acquiring The Taste* and *Three Friends* will each have lavish Steven Wilson remixes.

For now, on the CD we get three tracks from *Gentle Giant*, two from *Acquiring The Taste* and a further four from *Three Friends*, fleshed out with early track 'Freedom's Child' (previously heard on *Under Construction*) and the 7-inch mix of 'Nothing At All'. They sound amazing, and the *Three Friends* tracks especially show just how poorly served we've been by previous CD issues of this album.

It's the Blu-ray disc, however, that makes *Three Piece Suite* indispensable. The same tracks are remixed in 5.1 Surround and fans have been effusive about Wilson's skill at bringing out the revealing details of the instrumentation in this format. In addition, there are instrumental versions of the same tracks – karaoke, anyone? – as well as the entirety of all three albums transferred flat in 96/24 stereo LPCM, which means that as long as you've got an audiophile Blu-ray player, you can hear them sounding better than ever before. The package comes in a foldout digipack with a glossy booklet containing detailed liner notes by Anil Prasad, and featuring interviews with the band.

Unburied Treasure

The mother of all boxes, the very limited edition *Unburied Treasure*, released at the tail end of 2019, featured a cornucopia of Gentle Giant material, from the ephemeral, right through to the main course: each of the 12 albums newly remastered.

In addition, the box contains seventeen albums of live material, and the highlight: a hi-res Steven Wilson 5.1 remix of the debut *Gentle Giant* album on Blu-ray disc.

The package also includes a tour book and a biography, and replica posters.

Sadly, however, its price point and the limited quantities involved, made *Unburied Treasure* beyond the means of many fans.

Epilogue

You'd think that 50 years after their formation and 40 years after Gentle Giant put the lid on the genie, the group would be a distant memory. Instead, they're almost hip for the first time, and there's a genuine buzz about this odd group whose music has stood the test of time while standing out as decidedly different to anything contemporaneous or from any other era.

Punk, new wave and every subsequent new trend seemed to make the group more and more unpalatable to an audience versed on simplicity. The redemption of progressive rock over the past decade and the increasing interest in complex and 'difficult' music of all kinds, has now created an atmosphere where – perhaps for the first time – there's genuine curiosity about what the group were trying to do way back then, together with a willingness to understand it.

Go online, and it's not hard to find serious students of music attempting Gentle Giant songs in a variety of contexts, and some of them are outstanding. There's a new generation of musicians who aren't afraid of complex compositions and hellishly difficult time signatures, and for whom Gentle Giant's music presents a performative challenge that they can't resist. This, of course, rather confirms Gentle Giant's reputation as a group whose music is more appreciated by other musicians than by regular humans, but you only need look at the activity on the various social media pages and online forums and threads to see that year-by-year, interest in the group is only increasing.

So, why have there never been any reunions? It's almost unheard of in this era of nostalgia package tours for a band to remain completely schtum. One good reason was that by the time the group knocked it on the head, they'd given it their best shot and never anticipated a crescendo of interest 40 years later.

Derek gave it all up to become a successful record company executive, signing the likes of Bon Jovi, Tears For Fears, AC/DC and Jive Bunny (!). Brother Ray became a successful producer for the likes of The Sugarcubes, Ian McCullough, The Sundays and AR Kane, and latterly has become involved in writing music for computer games. Gary Green remained in the music scene but seems to have dabbled with various low-key projects. Likewise, Kerry Minnear has dabbled in music, reputedly playing keyboards at his wife's Methodist church, but has never again committed to a full-time band project. Instead, with his wife Lesley, he runs Alucard Music to administer all of Gentle Giant's business. John Weathers has been the most active post-Gentle Giant musician, as a member of Man until 1996 and various offshoots and other projects since. Sadly, he's more recently been fighting chronic ill-health.

The closest Gentle Giant has come to a reunion is the occasional Three Friends band, formed around Gary Green and Kerry Minnear in 2008 with Malcolm Mortimore on drums and originally boasting the rather fizzy mantle, Rentle Giant. The most recent lineup includes Neil Angilley (keyboards; Kerry left in 2009), Jonathan Noyce (Jethro Tull bassist), Mick Wilson (10cc vocalist) and Charlotte Glasson (multi-instrumentalist).

The group as a whole have, however, rejected all reunion offers, and it's not surprising considering that they're now pushing 70 and – in Derek's case especially – have been away from the performing aspects of the music scene for many years.

While the group's music is now, at last, being reanimated by at least some decent remastering work, there are also musicians and bands whose original music is clearly inspired by Gentle Giant, not the least of which is the London-based band Lost Crowns, a band giving a modern twist to the music we love so much.

Bibliography

Books
Stump, Paul., *Acquiring The Taste* (SAF Publishing, 2005)

Books On Progressive Rock That Include Material On Gentle Giant
Lucky, Gerry., *The Progressive Rock Files* (Collector's Guide, 1998)
Stump, Paul., *The Music's All That Matters* (Quartet, 1997)
Macan, Edward., *Rocking The Classics* (Oxford, 1997)

Online Resources
blazemonger.com – the official Gentle Giant website
wikiwand.com/en/Gentle_Giant – a Gentle Giant resource
https://lists.uoregon.edu/mailman/listinfo/on-reflection – Gentle Giant community
www.facebook.com/groups/GentleGiant/ – good unofficial public Gentle Giant page

On Screen series

Carry On... Stephen Lambe 978-1-78952-004-0

Powell and Pressburger Sam Proctor 978-1-78952-013-2

Seinfeld Seasons 1 to 5 Stephen Lambe 978-1-78952-012-5

Francis Ford Coppola Cam Cobb and Stephen Lambe 978-1-78952-022-4

Breaking Bad Roman Colombo 978-1-78952-045-3

Monty Python Steve Pilkington 978-1-78952-047-7

Other Books

Not As Good As The Book Andy Tillison 978-1-78952-021-7

The Voice. Frank Sinatra in the 1940s Stephen Lambe 978-1-78952-032-3

Maximum Darkness Deke Leonard 978-1-78952-048-4

The Twang Dynasty Deke Leonard 978-1-78952-049-1

Maybe I Should've Stayed In Bed Deke Leonard 978-1-78952-053-8

and many more to come!

Dream Theater - *on track*
every album, every song

Dream Theater - on track
every album, every song
Jordan Blum
Paperback
160 pages
41 colour photographs
978-1-78952-050-7
£14.99
USD 21.95

Every album produced by the world's best-known progressive metal band.

No other band has affected modern progressive metal as deeply or widely as American quintet Dream Theater. Formed at Berklee College of Music as Majesty in 1985 by guitarist John Petrucci, drummer Mike Portnoy, and bassist John Myung, the group has spent thirty years repeatedly pushing new boundaries and reinventing their identity. Although other acts – such as Queensrÿche and Fates Warning – paved the way for the prog-metal subgenre, Dream Theater were without doubt the first to meld influences from both metal and progressive rock into a groundbreaking blend of quirky instrumentation, extensively complex arrangements, and exceptional songwriting. Whether subtly or overtly, they've since left their mark on just about every progressive metal band that's followed.

In this book, Jordan Blum examines virtually all Dream Theater collections, and their behind-the-scenes circumstances, to explore how the group distinctively impacted the genre with each release. Whether classics of the 1990s like *Images and Words* and *Metropolis Pt. 2: Scenes from a Memory*, benchmarks of the 2000s like *Six Degrees of Inner Turbulence* and *Octavarium*, or even thrilling modern efforts like *A Dramatic Turn of Events* and *Distance Over Time*, every sequence of albums contributes something crucial to making Dream Theater's legacy nothing short of astonishing.

The Who - *on track*
every album, every song

The Who - on track
every album, every song
Geoffrey Feakes
Paperback
176 pp
42 colour photographs
978-1-78952-076-7
£14.99
USD 21.95

Every album produced by one of the world's best-selling - and most controversial - rock bands.

Formed in 1964 and still going strong in 2020, the Who are one of the most popular and enduring bands in the history of rock. The legendary debut album *My Generation* and a string of hit singles paved the way for Live At Leeds, hailed as the best live rock album of all time, and the best selling *Who's Next*. Powered by the phenomenal rhythm section of Keith Moon and John Entwistle, they earned a reputation as a premier live act and pioneered festival and arena performances. The rock operas *Tommy* and *Quadrophenia* took popular music into uncharted territories and both inspired hit films. Despite regular infighting, breakups and the death of two key members, the band continued into the 21st century with the well received *Endless Wire* album and original members Roger Daltrey and Pete Townshend stage spectacular live shows to this day.

This book examines each one of the band's studio albums, including the latest Who released in December 2019. Non-album tracks are also included and the book traces the band's long and diverse history. Compilations, live albums and soundtracks are also discussed, making this the most comprehensive guide to the music of the Who yet published. Whether the reader is a diehard fan or someone curious to see what lies beyond *Tommy*, this is essential reading.

10cc - *on track*
every album, every song

10cc and Godley and Creme -
on track
every album, every song
Peter Kearns
Paperback
176 pages
42 colour photographs
978-1-78952-054-5
US ISBN: 978-1-78952-075-0
£14.99
USD 21.95

**Every album
produced by this
cult British band -
and offshoot duo
Kevin Godley and
Lol Creme.**

Hailing from Manchester, England, sophisticated pop purveyors 10cc hit the ground running with their 1972 debut single, 'Donna'. Their pedigree reached back to bassist Graham Gouldman's '60s' songwriting successes including The Yardbirds' 'For Your Love' and The Hollies' 'Bus Stop'. Guitarist and recording engineer, Eric Stewart, was already a bonafide pop star having sung the global 1966 hit, 'Groovy Kind of Love', for his group The Mindbenders. When the pair teamed up with drummer/singer Kevin Godley and multi-instrumentalist/singer, Lol Creme, the combination wrought a legacy of four albums. They included the ambitious *The Original Soundtrack* and several hit singles, including the groundbreaking 'I'm Not In Love,' that were rich in eclectic boundary-pushing pop that earned 10cc comparisons to The Beatles while still occupying a unique position in music.

Departing in 1976, Godley and Creme moved on to create genre-defying experimental albums, while Gouldman and Stewart continued their run of hit singles and albums with a new 10cc lineup. Their final album was 1995's, *Mirror Mirror*, a highly respectable full stop on the influential band's colourful and innovative discography. This book examines every released recording by both Godley & Creme and 10cc, including the band's debut album under their early name, Hotlegs.

Mike Oldfield - *on track*
every album, every song

Mike Oldfield - on track
every album, every song
Ryan Yard
Paperback
176 pages
42 colour photographs
978-1-78952-060-6
£14.99
USD 21.95

**Every album
produced by one of
the most enigmatic
and talented solo
artists of the 1970s.**

It can be difficult for an artist to have such overwhelming success so early into their career as was the case for Mike Oldfield. To this day, his name is forever synonymous with the album *Tubular Bells*. Mike followed this album with three further long form works in the 1970s, before venturing off onto other musical paths. The 1980s saw further success both in the albums and singles charts, while recent years have seen a return to long form music, often via sequels to his most famous work, with his most recent album being *Return To Ommadawn* in 2017.

The music of Mike Oldfield touches listeners in ways that can be hard to describe. It bridges the gap between many musical cultures, whilst staying sharp and alert to current technological trends. In this book, Ryan Yard looks at the entire catalogue of albums to uncover what it is that makes his music so special. Each track from every album is critiqued with the aim of offering long term fans a different perspective whilst enticing new fans to explore and familiarise themselves with such wonderful new music. It makes a wonderful companion as the listener absorbs the music, hopefully offering food for thought as they embark on, or continue, their journey through the music of this remarkable artist.

Would you like to write for Sonicbond Publishing?

At Sonicbond Publishing we are always on the look-out for authors, particularly for our two main series:

On Track. Mixing fact with in depth analysis, the On Track series examines the work of a particular musical artist or group. All genres are considered from easy listening and jazz to 60s soul to 90s pop, via rock and metal.

On Screen. This series looks at the world of film and television. Subjects considered include directors, actors and writers, as well as entire television and film series. As with the On Track series, we balance fact with analysis.

While professional writing experience would, of course, be an advantage the most important qualification is to have real enthusiasm and knowledge of your subject. First-time authors are welcomed, but the ability to write well in English is essential.

Sonicbond Publishing has distribution throughout Europe and North America, and all books are also published in E-book form. Authors will be paid a royalty based on sales of their book.

Further details are available from www.sonicbondpublishing. co.uk. To contact us, complete the contact form there or email info@sonicbondpublishing.co.uk